Dancing with Time

José María R. Olaizola SJ

Translated by Helena Scott

Published by Messenger Publications, 2025

Bailar con el tiempo by José María R. Olaizola SJ © Editorial Sal Terrae, 2023 – Grupo de Comunicación Loyola, S. L. U. – Bilbao (Spain) / gcloyola.com

Translation copyright © Messenger Publications, 2025

ISBN: 9781788126953

Designed by Brendan McCarthy
Typeset in Garamond Premier Pro
Printed by Hussar Books

Messenger Publications,
Milltown Park, Dublin D06 W9Y7, Ireland
www.messenger.ie

Contents

Introduction

Have you ever found yourself feeling sorry when another birthday comes round? Do you think youth is the best stage of life? Do you think you ought to stay young forever? At twenty, do you talk about people of forty as if they were ancient? In your forties, do you talk about twenty-year-olds as if they were mere children? Do you find that the years are going by quicker and quicker? Then you need to learn to dance with time.

'Time is going by and we're starting to get old', as a ballad by Pablo Milanés starts off. He then laments the changes he finds, longs to get springtime back, mythifies the early stages of love and looks at his past youth with melancholy eyes, sorry to see how greyness and routine are taking over and killing his joys. How romantic! And also, how totally wrong! Time does go by, but it's not an enemy. It is, or it should be, an ally on the pathway of our lives.

Everyone's life has its own soundtrack; we all have an ongoing musical accompaniment to our lives. It's the music we have inside, which makes us vibrate, feel and act. It's composed of words, silences, songs, names, snatches of life. We each hear it in our own way and move to the sound of that inner tune that sometimes makes us jump for joy and other times makes us keep still. Yes, the music is now joyous, now sad; now triumphant, now desolate.

I love seeing people dancing. Some dances are well-rehearsed, each step is planned, and the dance follows a pattern created in advance. Maybe they're repetitive, but they do have their own beauty, charm, art, rhythm. They are no less lovely for being carefully studied; no less real for having been practised beforehand. I must admit, though, I prefer dancing that's improvised, spontaneous, that just seems to happen unexpectedly when people let themselves go and don't even know what's coming next. When people interact like that, you sometimes get to a point that surpasses anything you could imagine. And it's not just about dancing with other people; there are also solos. Lots of dances are danced on one's own, with nobody else, no interaction. You move, you escape, you express yourself just the way you are.

Not all dancing is external and physical. Lots of the things we do are a dance – lots of the conflicts, plenty of the needs we express, plenty of the anger and also plenty of the love. Much of the life we have inside us can also be described as a dance.

In short, I like to talk about life as a dance. A few years ago I wrote a short book on dancing with loneliness, and I was surprised and delighted at the number of people who identified with that. I think many more aspects of life can be described in some way as dancing. After all, we don't only dance with loneliness. We also dance with happiness, sadness, hope, love and so much more. We dance with people. That's what our story consists of. Friendship, suffering, tiredness, hurts, expectations, break-ups, reconciliations, what are all these but steps in the ongoing dance that is life? Words dance in the writer's imagination, and after-wards those words dance in the reader's imagination too. Writer and reader fill them with meaning, with what those words evoke for each of them, with memories either experienced or imagined. Even faith itself can be described as a dance with God and also with the others in the community.

One of the most universal dances of all is our interaction with time, because time is not something objective, scientifically measurable and the same for everyone. Maybe a particular dimension of time is; maybe, *pace* the theory of relativity, we can agree that one hour measures sixty minutes, one week measures seven days and one year measures three hundred and sixty-five days plus approximately six hours, and that's the same for everyone living in the same latitude. But there is something unique, undefined, subjective and personal in our relationship with time.

Time is one of the most important dimensions of life. How much revolves around it! Think about it for a moment. Insofar as time is limited, you have to choose what you're going to use it for. You choose to read this book, and you may be able to combine that with another activity like listening to music, but definitely not with watching a series on your favourite streaming platform – if you're trying to, please close it and centre yourself. We need to choose what to use time for because it's limited. That doesn't necessarily mean it's insufficient. When you've got lots of plans, myriad different jobs, looming deadlines and so many other things to do, obviously you're going to be short of time. But it can also happen that a single afternoon turns into an unending desert, hard to cross. Often, when someone is going through a hard time, telling them to be patient only adds to their discouragement! They're already finding that each minute stretches before them like an eternity. Yes, time is strange. Is it an ally or an aggressor, a friend or an enemy? Maybe all of them.

As you get older you realise more and more clearly how important the passage of time is. Perhaps because you've travelled more of the road, you have more memories and are carrying more baggage. Then you can compare things. You realise that years go by quicker than you thought, and having survived one or two crises helps you understand how fleeting life is. One day you're proud of having reached the age of twenty, and then almost before you realise it you've reached fifty, which, when you were young, seemed like extreme old age. What happened? How did you get there? Did the clocks suddenly speed up or what?! All that is part of life.

There can certainly be many ways of dancing with time. There's the dance of everyday life, with various different aspects – haste, patience, impatience, fragmentation, acceleration, memory, forgetting, calm … There are also the dances of each stage of life: childhood with all its learning processes, adolescence with its tensions and conflicts, young adulthood with its development, full adulthood with its coming down to earth, old age with its winter.

In this book I want to talk about one of the dances with time that comes into many life stories. It is the path that, all being well, leads us from youth into maturity. The singular process, unique for each person, of 'growing up', in the sense used by children when they talk about becoming adults one day, and what they want to be when they're grown-ups.

I don't think it's strictly a question of age, or at least not only, or mainly. I don't know if there's one specific age at which someone is a young person and another at which that same person is an adult. When exactly someone stops being a young person and starts being an adult seems to depend on the currents, dynamics and habits of the society they live in. Perhaps there was a time when you were an adult at twenty and were treated as such. Today, you continue being 'young' until you're thirty, and plenty of folk still self-identify as 'young people' well into their thirties and even beyond.

Being an adult means being somehow settled in life. It's the life you live when you take on responsibilities and put down roots. Obviously children or adolescents have their own share of responsibilities or ought to have. A good upbringing shouldn't remove that fact but empower it, because what we learn in childhood and early youth, we will develop on our own account later on. But an adult's responsibilities are no longer supervised by anyone else, and often there's no safety net if something goes wrong. Life is what it is.

It's hard work becoming an adult, hard but enthralling. It's even harder today, in this society that seems spellbound by the myth of eternal youth, and where Narcissus and Peter Pan play at meeting without ever growing older.

When writing about life, there's a constant danger of inventing rules. You start saying how things ought to be, you take yourself as a point of reference, and consciously or unconsciously you make your own reactions, ambitions and achievements – or at least the ones you're happy with – into the model of what other people's lives should be. But in fact every person's story is unique, so generalisations risk oversimplification, caricature and lack of due perspective. I'll try not to fall into this temptation. I hope to be able to offer a sufficiently broad and generally applicable approach.

Who is this book for? Mainly two sets of people. First of all, you young people. The following pages contain a proposal, a route-map, a description of the series of battles that make up a life. They aren't instructions. I can't tell you how or when those battles will arise in your specific circumstances. Each life is unique, as I say, and our processes and pathways are very different. Some people come to maturity very soon, by choice, necessity or a combination of the two, and there are others who still haven't quite achieved maturity even when their hair has gone white. But the process of becoming a mature person has some elements that are the same for almost everyone. Talking about it means sharing some lessons in case they're of any use to others. I don't claim to know all about your life, far from it, but I will offer something of what I've learnt in my own life, because I think it could be helpful.

The second set is you adults. Perhaps in the following pages, you, who have already left your youth behind or are still in it, may find a mirror of the processes you've lived through or are still going through. The battles I'll describe are ones we all have to fight. Sometimes you're keenly aware of the passing of time, sometimes you don't give it a thought. Sometimes your understanding of your lived experiences loses clarity or focuses more on wounds received than on all you've achieved. My proposal is for you to dialogue with your own story. Your love stories, the lessons of time, the discovery of your place in the world, the search for your calling, the names you carry with you, and the ones that are no longer there … Sometimes you'll see you were defeated. Other times you'll know you conquered. Perhaps you feel worn out after so many dances and battles, but despite it all, you're still going forward.

I want to talk, then, about fights and fears, about children who don't want to grow up and people who are making history, about the ways we see the past, the present and the future; about the temptation to fashion a world to our own liking, about seeing beyond our own selves, about how marvellous it is to put a name to our great desires and the challenge of defending them from the passage of time. I want to talk about the need to ask ourselves questions that lead us to think and choose.

I hope the dance is worthwhile.

1

Mythified Youth

Never before, perhaps, has youth been mythified to the extent it is today. Never before has it been so scrutinised, studied and stereotyped.

Sometimes I get invited to give a talk about 'young people today'. If no other information is included, I feel puzzled. Which young people are we talking about, which aspects of life? Wanting to measure them all by the same yardstick is like trying to catch the air and put it in a bottle. I'm not saying that such attempts aren't well intentioned. On the contrary, generalising probably produces clues that enable us to understand tendencies, interpret dynamics and propose pathways. If some level of generalisation weren't possible, this book would be meaningless, and my sociologist colleagues would have little scope for action in their attempts to understand and explain movements and social groups, but what is dangerous is to try generalising about such a broad population.

The temptation to put all young people in the same pigeonhole is nothing new. Maybe people have always done it. The twenty-first century did not invent the (often disapproving) phrase 'Young people today …' There is a quotation frequently, though spuriously, attributed to Socrates, which says, 'Children now love luxury; they have bad manners, contempt for authority; they show disrespect for their elders and love chatter instead of exercise. Children are now the tyrants, not the servants, of their households. They no longer rise when their elders enter the room. They contradict their parents, chatter before company, gobble up dainties at the table, cross their legs and tyrannise their teachers.'

This quotation may not have originated in classical antiquity, but people uncritically accept that it did, reflecting a general perception that each generation tends to exaggerate the defects of the following one.

'*We* were never like that' is a phrase frequently on the lips of anyone whose past memories are beginning to be equal in length to their probable future. '*We* lived through the post-war years.' '*We* stood up for democracy.' '*We* took those famous school exams.' '*We* used to play in the street.' '*We* weren't spoiled kids.' '*We* always respected our elders.' '*We* didn't spend the whole day glued to a screen.' Each generation seems eager to distance itself from the upcoming one, and comparisons beginning '*We* …' almost always imply that *we* were better.

Although that kind of generalisation has existed for ages, I would dare to say that in the twenty-first century youth is being mythified in a different way. Today criticism is mingled with envy. Everyone wants to be 'young': teenagers, because they want to get there; young people themselves, because they've arrived at the fabled stage that is so full of new experiences and possibilities; older people, because our society panics at the idea of getting older, very often associated with being 'elderly', as though getting old were something bad, and as though in any case there wasn't a very long stage (in fact the longest) to live through first: adult life. As though, 'If you don't want to feel old, you have to feel young.'

Two trends come together in this mythification of being young. First, we are bombarded with images of idyllic, impossibly beautiful young people, with perfect bodies, in idealised surroundings of flowers, trees, hills and blue skies. Secondly, the cosmetics industry promises to supply us with youthful looks that, if not actually permanent, can at least maintain the fiction of freshness until a very advanced age.

Many real young people, with real problems and real needs, are the first to be brought close to despair by this mythification. They are the ones who have to fight their way through the real difficulties of adult life, who know how hard it is to get a job that will give them independence, who would like to start a family but can't afford to, who sometimes have to fight to stop being treated like teenagers, who know that their love life is nothing like the carefree promiscuity of some television series whose whole cast seem to be engaged in constant bed-hopping. These young people are the first victims of the myth.

There are all sorts of generalisations and myths about young people – sociological, psychological and religious. Are they more conservative, more progressive, more polarised? Daydreamers and idealists? Materialists? Digital natives living in a virtual world? These and other attributes are often bandied about. Broadly speaking there are two categories of generalisation: condemning them and defending them. Both are unnecessary, and both are false, because among young people there's something of everything: progressives and conservatives, whatever those two labels may mean, extremists and centrists, dogmatists and relativists, hedonists and minimalists. Some read, and some don't. Some are promiscuous to the last degree, and some aim for stable, faithful relationships. Some are believers, and some are atheists. That said, it's true that one can easily hear and fall into all kinds of generalisations.

Condemnation exaggerates everything that is wrong with 'young people today'. According to those who join in this chorus of disapprobation, young people are materialistic, selfish, indisposed to fight for anything worthwhile, fickle, insensitive, incapable of forming strong relationships, promiscuous, rebellious, lazy, lacking in firm values, easily swayed, alienated by living in a digital world, incapable of keeping promises, enslaved by the present, given to hedonism and machismo, uninterested in the welfare of society or the common good, ill-mannered, and poorly-educated as a result of the deteriorating education system. These kinds of often-repeated generalisations could continue for several pages, and they are absurd. Because in reality there are certainly some young people like that. Likewise, there are young people who couldn't be further removed from that description, while there are older adults who match it down to the last detail.

The opposite extreme is mythifying and idealising young people. With a mix of patronising paternalism and pseudo-nostalgia, people praise everything 'young' to the skies with all sorts of epithets. According to this view, young people are tolerant, and much more welcoming to difference and diversity than their elders. They're idealistic; they dream great dreams and aim for a more just world; they are spiritual, concerned for the environment, and are the best-educated generation in history; they refuse to repeat their parents' lives because they want to break free from the treadmill of work and to enjoy life more and better; they're liberated, not chained to convention or tradition, and they don't put chains on love either; they use technology to broaden their world-view; they are creative, happy and freed from conventionalism. Once again, these are pointless generalisations. Are some young people like that? Certainly. Are all of them like that? Absolutely not. And again, there are older people who have many or all of the above characteristics.

Possibly older adults, including myself, tend to emphasise the negative, partly as a result of idealising our own youth. Perhaps a certain degree of nostalgia is inevitable when we recall those years when we were approaching adulthood but not yet weighed down by the responsibilities we would acquire with the passing of time. When wrinkles, or baldness, or extra kilos arrive, you remember yourself in the past as youthful, fresh-looking and fit – perhaps more so than you ever were in reality. When your days are stamped by routine, and the years stop being marked in the calendar by goals achieved or significant steps you'd been aiming at for a long time that imply ambitions fulfilled … you recall the time when you had so many possibilities ahead of you to choose from. In many cases people mythify youth as a way of not losing it completely. 'I'm still young', 'I still feel young', 'Being young is about how you see yourself, not how long ago you were born' – all of these betray a reluctance to face the fact that 'I've grown older'. And such people's self-deception is fed by the promises of eternal youth readily to hand – from cosmetics that promise a youthful appearance, to the care of the body, to the assurances offered by science that the aging process can be overcome and even reversed.

Added to all this is the proliferation of discourses that identify commitment with being trapped, praise a life with no roots and claim that anything that weighs you down, however momentarily, is a chain that you should break. All those things are part of life.

2

What Would You Tell
Your Younger Self?

We often talk about what lies ahead of us. We wonder where life is taking us. And our ideas include hopes, fears, the goals we've set ourselves and the unknowns. Perhaps youth is the time when we plan huge projects. Then our horizons narrow, as life comes down to earth and takes root, but anyway we don't stop dreaming of the future and imagining things otherwise. Often, too, we look back, especially when there's a long stretch of life already behind us.

You can learn a lot by looking back at your younger self. Some years ago, in a series of articles for a digital project, we suggested to a group of people that they should write a letter to their younger selves. The results were fascinating – the differences between them and also their agreement on certain questions. Their dialogues with their remembered selves brought back fears, life lessons and advice they would give themselves on how to avoid certain traps. And although it was a somewhat nostalgic exercise, based on an impossible premise, what came out of it were some notable lessons for adult life. Their advice was no longer any use to them, because their younger selves weren't there anymore. We can't protect the person we once were from the mistakes or traps we were going to make or fall into, nor from the unexpected and sometimes wounding trials that awaited us at some stage along the way. But perhaps this exercise can be useful to us now as a reminder of how much we have learned and to other people who still have to fight those battles.

We need a fairly clear head to be able to look at that younger self without indulging in useless regrets or self-reproach. We can't blame ourselves for not knowing then what we know now. Nor can we stop that younger self from making some decisions which, with the knowledge we now have, we wouldn't make today. If there were any way of going back in time, of course we might change one or two things. We may feel sorry we missed the chance to live a freer, happier life, instead of worrying so much over things that seemed overwhelming at the time. Daring to look back may even be painful. We know that in many areas there is no way of turning back. But despite all that, the backward glance is valuable as an overview of the steps taken up until now and as enabling us to recognise what our life has taught us.

Some months ago, I was much struck by an interview that the journalist Diane Sawyer had with Matthew Parry, one of the six stars of *Friends*, the famed 1990s American sitcom. The series was basically a number of rite-of-passage stories from youth to adulthood – like the later ones, *How I Met Your Mother* and *The Big Bang Theory*. In the interview with Sawyer, Perry reviewed his own life, with special emphasis on his descent into the world of addiction because he had been unable to stand the pressure of fame. At one point in the interview, seeing himself in a scene from the series, filmed during a time when he looked incredibly thin as a result of the addictions he was prey to, Perry made a painful confession.

> Of course it's very hard to watch that. Because in this weird way I feel sorry for that guy. Because that's a guy that's out of control. I didn't know what was going on with me. I weighed a hundred and fifty-five pounds, on my way to a hundred and twenty-eight pounds. I feel too sorry for that guy, he's going through too much, and … it's me.

He went on to explain the meaning of returning to those places in the past. It wasn't just a sterile or pathetic exercise. 'But whenever I was writing the book' – his autobiography – 'and I came to a section that was hard, I just thought however deep it went for me and dark it went for me, that will help somebody who got that dark. And I kept going.'[1]

---

1. ABC News, 'While soaring in fame, Matthew Perry says life was "out of control"', interview with Diane Sawyer, 29 October 2022, at 7:22, www.youtube.com/watch?v=yElaJSXGdqw

Looking at our past is a learning opportunity, for ourselves and other people, and a very valuable one. Okay, it can sometimes be painful to go back to places where we were unhappy, lost, where we even find it hard to recognise ourselves, but that ability to look back at the person we were then, from what we know now, without self-blame or self-deception, speaks of maturity, of paths travelled, of lessons learned. And it is also an exercise we can do at many points in life. The teenager can speak to the child. The twenty-year-old can speak to the teenager. The adult can speak to the young person. The older person can speak to the adult, who does not realise just how much still lies ahead. Some time ago I said in a post on the web:

> Sometimes you'd like to sit down with the person you were years back and tell them what you know now, and tell them not to be afraid to live, make mistakes and take risks ... Tell them to love themselves more, and then they'll be able to love other people better. Tell them that there are lots of battles that you don't win until you accept that they will always be there. And other battles that you win when you face up to them. And then, one way or another, those things stop having power over you. Tell them that God is much greater than they have any idea of right now, and they'll discover him progressively without realising it. You'd like to tell your younger self that wounds heal over. You wouldn't talk to them about some people who haven't yet come on the scene, or some who will always be there, perhaps so as not to spoil the discovery and the surprise of such rich friendships. You'd tell them to try not to make a drama out of some set-backs. To smile more. You'd advise them to watch their back, but they wouldn't pay much heed, because there are times when one believes one will stay young forever. And maybe that's a good thing.

It's a good exercise to sit down with the person you once were and tell them about the path that brought you here.

Perhaps the whole of this book is really a description of some of those possible lessons, mine and other people's. Lessons that we understand when we look back and see how far we've come. As adults we can dialogue with the younger self we left behind and finally come to understand the path we have travelled.

As well as this, young people should have a conversation at some stage with the adult they want to become. Here the journey is different, because there are no certainties but, at best, wishes and hopes. The problem comes when those hopes are over-narrow or just the opposite, too utopian. But there is something courageous about imagining where you want to go and daring to think about the steps you need to take today to get there.

Maybe when we talk to our past self, lots of different aspects of our life come to the surface: names, events, lessons, unexpected turns in the road … I like to say that we can forewarn them about some of the battles that await them, which they may be already fighting, sometimes unconsciously.

It's great when we can talk to them about the outcome, when we can assure them that there is light at the end of some of the tunnels they'll have to pass through. Our dance with time is indeed a dance, and it's also a battle. Both at once. In the next few chapters I aim to describe some of those dances and battles.

3

Battling with Fear

Out of all the battles I'm going to describe, the most ferocious one is probably the battle against fear. It's the one that has the greatest number of different facets and affects the most aspects of our lives. Becoming an adult involves facing up squarely to fear. Not an easy thing to do. Watching horror films and seeing the hero paralysed with fear, how often have we felt like yelling at them to move, run, *do* something! But they're frozen with fear, defenceless in the face of danger. The problem isn't being afraid. The problem is when we let fears stop us from living our lives.

You've probably heard of agoraphobia, a condition that turns people into recluses and prevents them from leaving their houses for fear of crowds or open spaces. Their only option is compulsive self-isolation, but it's obviously not a good solution. One wishes they could somehow overcome their sense of panic and go out into the open air. OK, but I think in some way we all need to overcome the temptation to isolate ourselves or shut ourselves away from … something.

Admit it, we can all remember being frightened as children. We've all felt insecure, lain awake at night, when we had to face something unpredictable and didn't know if we could cope.

In the series about advice people would give to their younger selves I mentioned in the last chapter, I think the most frequent recommendation, the piece of advice repeated most often when all those men and women were talking to their younger selves was, 'Don't be afraid.' What does that mean? It means that all of them – like all of us – remembered feeling afraid when they were young.

Fear doesn't belong to just one stage of life. There are the fears of childhood, adolescence, youth and adulthood. Probably we will all retain different fears until the last day of our lives. What's more, in many cases fear isn't just understandable; it's reasonable and prudent. Not seeing the seriousness of some threats can lead straight to disaster.

You'll surely have heard or read that courage isn't the absence of fear, it's the ability to master fear. And a coward is not someone who's afraid, but someone who doesn't dare face up to the danger, who gives in without a struggle.

Fear has many different causes. As we become progressively more aware of what life is like, and all the things that could go wrong, how can we avoid sometimes picturing ourselves in worst-case scenarios?

So what's really meant by the advice, 'Don't be afraid', offered by an adult to his or her past self? Does it mean that they've overcome all their fears and are now living confident, fear-free lives? Does being an adult mean banishing all spectres, living without any worries? Far from it!

We know that we will live with fears, in the plural, all our lives. What time and our own story give us are the perspective and experience to be able to face them. Young people have to face their fears without so much of either. It's not about capacity but opportunity. Many younger people haven't yet, perhaps, experienced failure, loss, rejection or defeat; and all those experiences, properly processed, become life lessons.

When someone looks back and says to their past self, 'Don't be afraid', they're not saying that everything's going to work out well or that those remembered fears were unfounded or imaginary, nor are they promising a life of safety, unassailed by any conflict or disappointment. Maybe there is someone who found that life went smoothly, and the only thing they want to tell their younger self is that a radiant future awaits them. But most of us who have lived a few decades know that joys and sadnesses were waiting for us that we never suspected back then. We know that some of the dreams we nursed on the threshold of adulthood popped like soap-bubbles, leaving us suffering a fair dose of pain. We know that some of the things we feared when young never actually materialised, while along the way there appeared other difficulties that made us more aware of how fragile everything is.

When we tell ourselves, 'Don't be afraid', what we're really saying is, 'Don't let fear paralyse you.' That's the whole point. If we hold back from doing certain things, from taking some important decisions, from setting off along particular paths that lie before us, for fear that something may go wrong, perhaps we're protecting ourselves from the outcome, but probably we're also refusing to live. We have to confront our fears, and not in a pretence that everything will go well. Everything won't go well. We may crash. Our worst nightmares may come true.

What you learn in adulthood is that it wasn't such a big deal after all. We can see this by taking another look at the most frequent fears young people feel. Let's think about three of the worst: fear of failure, fear of rejection and fear of loneliness.

Fear of failure

Under this heading I could also talk about fear of the future, because the two go hand in hand. The root of this fear is realising how many things can go wrong. When we're little, and if we have the immense good luck to have a home and a protective family, we can spend years in happiness and security. The sharper edges of life may be hidden from us. Death is something that happens in films. And if the adults in your life encounter failure they conceal it, not because they want to lie to you, but because they want to protect you. Parents do their best to give their children a sense of security for as long as they can. They don't weigh them down with money problems. If they quarrel, they try to do it in private. They don't tell the children how ill grandad is until it's unavoidable, and so on.

It's true that as you start growing up, you're forced to realise that life isn't an easy journey along a pre-determined route with everything set out and guaranteed in writing. While you're still young, you begin to discover that life is an obstacle-race. That you have to set yourself targets and achieve them, in many different aspects of life. And as you start looking to the future, your own future, plenty of questions come up about all you need to obtain, all you have to prove. As a student, you have to pass exams. In sport, you want to win. On social networks, you need to get yourself noticed. If you're aiming for a popular university course, you have to get an offer of a place. You need to hunt for a job or go in for a competitive exam. At some point you'll need to settle down. Will you achieve independence? Will anyone love you? The questions get more and more acute. What if you don't manage? What if you fail in the projects you set up? What if you can't earn the money you need? What if you don't live up to your family's expectations? What if nobody falls in love with you?

These and other questions are enough to make anyone dizzy. They're scary. I'm sure that if we asked all those adults who look back on their younger selves what they were afraid of back then, they would answer with lots of variations on those same fears of failure on their path to the future.

There are certain ways of dealing with these fears that offer false security. They look like a way out, but it's a trick – although they may calm you down, in fact they just lock you into your youthful state of indecision.

The first of these false solutions is short-termism. To avoid being terrified of the future, just don't think about it. Don't set yourself long-term goals, because you might not succeed. Lower your expectations. Don't dream. Enjoy today, secure in what you've got here and now, and don't suffer needlessly. All of this may make you feel better, but basically it imprisons you within closed horizons, in the present. Later on we'll get to talk about the importance of the present moment. It's something we have to respect, but it isn't everything.

Another false solution is superficial feel-good optimism. It comes in all those self-help resources and narratives that repeat endlessly how you shouldn't fear failure because you're not going to fail. You only need to do a quick search online to find every kind of upbeat motto designed to banish all shadows and insecurities: 'Dream big!' 'Shine like the jewel you really are!' 'If you want it badly enough, you'll get it.' 'Happiness is an inside job.' 'You are your own favourite place.' 'Dreams come true when you believe in them!' 'Life's a wonderful journey.' 'If you put your heart into it, if you're truly determined, if you don't give in, if … then you'll triumph!'

I think all of that is feasible as a motivational strategy, and it can have its uses in helping people not to throw in the towel and concede defeat. But as a description of real life, it's just a hoax. Obviously, there are certain things that, however hard you try, you're not going to achieve. I can train as hard as I like, but I'll never be a Michael Phelps. I can do a thousand art courses, but Michelangelo's genius wasn't just a matter of technique. Motivation is fine, but it shouldn't be used to hide reality. Sometimes you try as hard as you possibly can, and yet you fail.

The third false solution is typical of our times. To avoid failure, let's just delete the concept of failing. This often occurs in discussions about education. Let's get rid of qualifications. No one will ever have to repeat a year. Let's tell everyone they're brilliant. 'You study so well!' 'You write so well!' 'You sing so well!' 'You're so funny on TikTok!' 'You've got such a lovely smile!' Let's rate everything as equally good, and then everyone will feel appreciated.

I'm not saying we shouldn't help everyone to feel valued and discover their abilities, but that can't be done at the price of eliminating goal-setting, demands and the real possibility of failure. We shouldn't imagine that telling someone they've failed a test is counter-productive or think that success and failure oughtn't to exist. They do exist. Therefore we need to help people learn to cope with success without getting bigheaded and with failure without being overwhelmed by a single defeat.

Obstacles on life's path are being removed so that people can go forward. In itself this sounds like a good thing, and in many cases yes, it needs to be done, but there is a trap. However much we try to smooth the path, life does go through rough patches. There will be trips, blows and falls. The only thing you achieve by being over-protective is to create people with a false sense of security, who are absolutely unable to cope with difficulties, who are convinced that the world revolves around them and can't bear the idea that there are areas of reality that will never adapt to suit their convenience.

So where does the battle against the fear of failure start? What can be done? Sow a seed by facing up to this fear, recognising the fact that failing is not the worst thing that can happen. In fact, sooner or later you will fail. Of course you will, and so will everyone. One of your dreams won't come true. You'll stake something on a cherished project and lose it. You'll be cheated of one or other of your ambitions. Maybe after fighting for a long time for a particular position, the time will come when you decide to give up. Perhaps it will take you longer than you expected to find a job that fulfils you, or it may cost you a titanic effort to achieve independence. Maybe at some point someone will break your heart, or you may break it yourself, because you hadn't learned how to love. All those things can happen, and in fact at least some of them probably will happen somewhere along the way.

What you discover as you grow up is that contrary to what you once believed, you do survive failures, you do pick yourself up after a fall. Maybe it takes time, maybe you carry the bruises for a while, maybe after picking yourself up your pace is a bit slower, a bit more painful, and it's hard to recover the swiftness you lost. Maybe the wounds leave scars as a permanent reminder of the thing that went wrong. But you really are much stronger than you imagine, much more resilient. And life is more complex. Doors are shut, and windows open. You miss some trains, and others come along. Dreams are left behind, and before you know where you are, the dreamer is at it again, creating new ones.

Secondly, fear of the future can't be overcome by refusing to look ahead and installing yourself in a pretended 'absolute present'. It's overcome by asking yourself what step you can take here and now to get where you want to be. In other words, winning in the future begins today. You have to fight for it, obviously. Life necessarily includes an element of battling, overcoming obstacles, setting goals.

It would be dishonest to assure you that if you start today, you'll definitely achieve your goal. Maybe you won't. Maybe you'll fail and will have to begin again. But it's even more certain that if you don't begin to lay the foundations today, you'll never build anything stable in the future and will spend your life dodging between different baseless options that last about as long as a mood.

Fear of rejection

I'd like to introduce this section by referring to a film that made quite an impact recently. It's *The Banshees of Inisherin*. The starting point is surprising. In a little village on a remote island off the west coast of Ireland, after being friends all their lives, Pádraic one day finds that Colm has decided to end their friendship. No explanation, no apparent reason. All their cordiality and warmth has turned into distance. The evenings spent sharing beers and talking in the village pub are a thing of the past, replaced by Colm's flat rejection of all his erstwhile bosom friend's attempts to get near him. The more relentless and crushing Colm's rejection is, the more Pádraic redoubles his efforts to recover their lost affection, because it's really hard to cope with being rejected. Their strange, tormented relationship highlights many elements of real life. Affection, distance, incomprehension, inequality in friendship, inability to cope with the frustration of not being loved ... Without giving any spoilers, I have to say that it's not a predictable friends-falling-out story, with dramatic developments leading up to a happy ending. Is it aiming to work as a metaphor for our times, for the breakdown in communication, the absence of friendship or family ties? Is it, as I read somewhere, an allegory for the Irish Civil War? A dark story about the strange connection between hope and bitterness? There's all of that in it, but above all it offers a plain fact: how really hard it is to accept rejection by someone else. Yet if you refuse to accept it, it can drive you mad.

So this is another fear that can take root when we're young: fear of rejection. We want people to accept us, approve of us, like us, admire us. We want to fit in. However loved and secure we felt when we were little, however many talents, abilities and values we have, and however likeable we really are, in adolescence all kinds of insecurities can start to grow in us, and we can feel thoroughly ill-adjusted, and can go through a stage of disliking ourselves.

We can cover it up, hide it all behind a false attitude of security, mask all our self-doubt behind a pretence of self-confidence. Without want-ing to generalise, I wonder whether that is why young people so often lay down the law, talk in absolute terms, try to give the impression that they have much clearer ideas than they really do, and judge others so harshly. They don't really think like that, but they're afraid to show any weakness. They need to seem strong, out of a fear that if they show themselves to be weak, fragile or limited, then others will reject them. They think that in order to be liked, they have to show their strengths and hide their weaknesses. As simple as that.

Added to all this today is the pressure of being judged publicly. The moment you have a social media account you are being evaluated. People measure you up, scrutinise the little details, make comments on what you do, your features, your shape and size, your friends, your leisure, your words and your silences. They 'like' you or reject you publicly, for everyone in the world to see. They praise you and insult you. Comparison with others is an ever-present temptation. Popularity can be minutely quantified. And so can rejection.

OK, what I've just said is a huge generalisation, and it's easy to fall into stereotyping. But something like that does happen. It's nothing new. What *is* new is possibly the expansion of social networks as a space for endlessly multiplying interaction and exposure.

We naturally want to be liked and appreciated. We want to be accepted. We find it hard to cope with rejection, or criticism, no matter which direction it comes from.

When we realise we've been rejected there are three possible reactions. One is to look for someone to blame, which must be either the person who rejects us, or our own selves or a third party who we think has caused the rejection. If we blame the person who rejects us, we set up a barrier and reject them in our turn, generating conflicts. If we blame ourselves, we fall into self-reproach and try to reverse the situation, especially when we aren't capable of simply accepting it. If we look for a third party to blame, we risk stirring up further ongoing ill-feeling and suspicion.

A second reaction is to try desperately to change the rejection into acceptance. This feels especially urgent when you're rejected by people who matter to you. I'm not saying it shouldn't be attempted sometimes. Not every relationship that goes off track is impossible to repair. The world of connections and affections is so complex that no two relationships are alike. What's more, in some circumstances it is important that even if there's no friendship, there should at least be respect and tolerance. Just imagine having to spend years working with people who are your declared enemies. Terrible.

That said, a mature way of reacting involves recognising that sometimes the only option is to accept the distance. We can't be liked by everyone. Let's pause for a moment on that fact. Not everyone will find us likeable. This is not about being objective. The world of liking and friendship is not subject to rational analysis. What attracts one person, another person finds off-putting. Sometimes you meet someone and for no known reason you get on well from the start. Other times there is distance and antipathy, maybe reciprocated, from the word go. And you can't find any objective explanation or apparent reason. It's no one's fault. And it's no big deal. Just as you don't find everyone immediately likeable, the opposite is also true.

So maybe the mature thing to do is try and be faithful to what you really are. Don't aim to please the people who reject you but to nurture the relationships that support you, build you up and give your life some meaning, because that's key. We can't be liked by everyone, but on the other hand, normally we aren't disliked by everyone. The proverb, 'There's a lid for every pot', really does apply here, meaning that there are like-minded people for everyone, so that what is frankly off-putting for some, others will find completely irresistible.

Think for a moment about the people you know. How often have you been surprised by the unexpected ways different people connect? Unpredictable friendships, people with whom you can't think of anything to talk about but who spend hours chatting to each other about things they find interesting and amusing. People you'd never have imagined getting together, who end up living happily ever after. The fact is there are always people who have things in common.

The key is to discover the people in your life who can become real points of reference for you, and then take every opportunity of making really good friends with them, perhaps establishing family ties and working on shared projects, or simply knowing that they're there.

Life is too short to waste time on trying to get people to like you if they don't. There's no reason to do that. Less still to spend time and energy lamenting your rejection by someone. In many cases the best remedy for falling out with someone is to keep a healthy distance.

Fear of loneliness

I've already written in depth about this aspect of life in *Dancing with Loneliness*,[2] but it's still worth going back over the topic. Young people also have to battle with their share of loneliness, and it's different from the loneliness experienced at other ages. It isn't adolescent anguish, middle-aged boredom or the diminishing powers of old age. For young people who are emerging into adult life, one of the biggest challenges is finding love; and it isn't easy. Our first loves, almost always experienced in extreme youth, when everything is being discovered for the first time, are usually intense, overwhelming, sometimes agonising. We get lifted up into the clouds, and every one of the emotions that are awakened in the course of our relationship is felt passionately. The first time we say, 'I love you', and the first time we hear and believe it; the first kiss; so many firsts. First loves are intense, romantic affairs, whether the person concerned is the most emotional person in the world or very much on the rational side. Sometimes that first love takes root, and as the years go by it becomes a life project. In such cases, coming to maturity means learning to move on from the happy early stages to days that are, well, more everyday. Other times, a first love is followed by a first disappointment, and the feeling that nothing will ever be the same again. The Spanish group La Oreja de Van Gogh sang, 'Your first love is the only one that's true … the others just help you forget what you knew'. That may be a bit of an exaggeration, but the fact is that at some stage in life you start to be afraid that true love is impossible, or at least love as you once imagined it, dreamed of it, perhaps mythified it.

---

2. J. M. Rodríguez Olaizola SJ, *Dancing with Loneliness* (Dublin: Messenger Publications, 2023).

Overcoming our fear of never finding love is also part of the path to maturity.

We can learn how to love. Oddly enough, in the course of our lives we are given training in all kinds of things. We start learning lessons when we are very small: formal and informal education, support classes, sports, language lessons, social skills, singing lessons, how to play a musical instrument, driving lessons, cookery lessons. Before you know it, primary-school children are putting on aprons and concocting haute cuisine delicacies you don't even know the names of. Believers go to catechism classes to learn the basics of the faith. You can sign up for all kinds of courses: photography, how to become an influencer, filters, publishing, cosmetics ... creative writing workshops for future novelists, bitcoin sessions for aspiring millionaires. Training courses are offered on all kinds of topics. A law was passed in Spain recently, requiring anyone who wants to get a pet to take a course first on how to look after it properly. A list of all the different types of learning would fill pages and pages.

If all these things have to be learned, why would we not need to learn how to love? Of course we do, but there are no lessons, no courses and no qualifications in this subject. I don't want to put that idea into anyone's head, in case some bright spark with nothing better to do at the Department for Education decides that the government needs to tell us what love consists of. It wouldn't surprise me, the way things are going. I can see it becoming yet another ideological weapon for various globalisers, who recommend polyamory and exalt egoism with equal fervour.

Perhaps one's own life and the example of people we trust are the best schools for learning how to love. Let's hope we're capable of growing in wisdom, learning lessons from the events and actions of our lives, learning from our successes and from our mistakes, and learning to give a name to love. You learn in your times of self-giving, in little acts that become a seed that will bear fruit in due season. You learn that sometimes you need to talk and other times to respect someone's silence. You learn that you cannot possess anyone, and that sometimes means that you have to lose, and let them walk away. You learn by getting things wrong. There are things that you'd do differently if you had another chance – but you haven't. You also learn from unforgettable moments that are engraved on your memory and from unpleasant episodes that may leave scars. On the path towards real love, you start to understand certain truths about yourself and other people.

Love isn't just an emotion, though it does include emotions. Adolescents are tempted to think feelings and emotions are the same thing as truth. For many people today 'what I feel' becomes the ultimate standard for judging what is right. If I feel it, it's right. If I don't feel it, it's false and wrong. But love can't depend wholly on feelings. Feelings have their times, their ebb and flow. You won't be in the same mood forever. Love has to put down roots, so that when at any stage your feelings may be confused or slacken off, or even seem to point in other directions, there are also your convictions, your will, your reason, the things that previously motivated you to commit your life to one person. Real, mature love goes much deeper than mere emotions.

Love isn't a succession of eternal present moments. The true meaning of *carpe diem*, 'seize the day', will be discussed a bit later on in this book. For now, all I will say is that one of the most amazing discoveries involved in becoming an adult is that time flies. It passes quickly; the present is not eternal, and today doesn't last. You progressively add more and more experiences to your biography, and you pass through stages and attain goals that once seemed so far distant that they didn't even seem worth taking into account. You have to decide whether love is going to be a mere collection of purely present moments, in which case it will not become a true story, or if you really want to write love stories with your life. Love stories that will be built up on what you have experienced (the past), what you are experiencing now (the present) and what you hope your life will be (the future).

With apologies to Plato and his world of pure ideas, love is not an idea. If we are believers, perhaps our faith enables us to glimpse in God a love that includes everything good: a love that is eternal, faithful, detached, generous, compassionate, fruitful, untiring ... and all the characteristics that we can intuit in God. But we are a fairly imperfect reflection of that love. The Chilean musician, singer and Jesuit Cristóbal

Fones said, 'If I were to give some advice to my younger self, I would start by inviting myself to put more determination into loving what is imperfect.'[3] I don't think it could be put better or more concisely. Some young people are ambitious, dreamers, demanding on themselves and other people. They aim high. They seek perfection in many spheres of life. They demand perfection of themselves, and also of their parents, the Church, the institutions they belong to … and their partners. And so sometimes they have to cope with a mixture of frustration about what is not perfect and their ambition to achieve perfection. Young people have the right to aspire to great heights, but they also need, as they go forward, to discover and accept the fact that reality is more limited. That doesn't mean surrendering or giving in to pessimism. It doesn't mean that life is horrible and reality will always let you down. It means accepting that reality is imperfect, and so are we, and so is love, but we can love what is imperfect. In fact, maybe that's what true love is: learning to share lights and shadows, finding the sort of person with whom we can lower our guard, realising that there is someone else who knows about our inner torment and is ready to tackle it with us, and learning to have that same attitude towards the imperfections and limitations of the person we love.

Another lesson follows on from that. Love doesn't mean collecting a set of perfect moments when everything works out well; it means writing true stories. If love includes what is imperfect, then it also includes mistakes, wounds, disappointments, complicated episodes, misunderstandings and bad times. Just as it also includes successes, caresses, joys, sheer delight, happy encounters and thoroughly good times. But love is all of that, both nights of torment and radiantly sunny days.

Love is not a mirror for gazing at our own reflection. That might be one of the things we most need to learn: how to change from thinking the world revolves around us to focusing more on other people than ourselves. Learning to give up something when someone we love needs it. Love is not looking in the mirror of the other in order to see how good

---

3. C. Fones, *'De proyectos y logros que pasan, rostros y nombres que quedan'*, pastoralsj.org, https://pastoralsj .org/ser/1894-de-proyectos-y-logros-que-pasan-y-rostros-y-nombres-que-quedan.

we are. It is looking at the other and discovering them as someone we love, someone we're ready to make sacrifices for. The clearest example of this – obviously not the only one – is parents' love for their children. How often the fact of having a child changes everything! It may be the first time that people experience a readiness to give absolutely freely. As fathers and mothers, you will see how your lives are changed with the arrival in them of children whom you love more than you would have thought possible. Timetables stop being shaped to suit you and instead fit in with the needs of a completely helpless newborn baby who depends entirely on you, and for whom you're ready to do without so many things that up until then seemed essential and non-negotiable. True love is love that has learned to give and to give itself.

To sum up, as a conclusion for this chapter, fear is part of life. When we tell ourselves not to be afraid, what we're really doing is telling ourselves not to let fear paralyse us. Being afraid is part of being human. Maybe the adolescent fears we've just looked at will stay with us all our lives. Maybe we'll overcome them and others will appear. Adult life has its own labyrinths and threats: fears of losing what we've achieved, fears for our children in a world like today's with so many things that can go horribly wrong, fears of sickness and death, which for so many years never bothered us because they seemed so far off and we felt invulnerable. There's nothing wrong with being concerned, but we have to live.

4

Battling with Peter Pan

In search of eternal youth

Can you imagine being able to halt the effects of time and stay young forever? Can you imagine being able to 'freeze' your life at an age when you had all the strength of youth and none of the duties and burdens of being an adult? The fact is that just asking the question reveals that there are two very different answers, plus a whole range of possible variations in between. At one end there would be people who are horrified at the thought of it. Who on earth would want to live like that? Who would want to get stuck in that kind of loop? Surely a time would come when you got tired of being permanently young – eternal youth would become a prison, where sameness and boredom took over from what had earlier been novelty and entertainment! And at the other end, people who would jump at the chance. Why would anyone want to grow into an adult? Why should you want to leave behind the age of myriad possibilities and embark on the daily grind? Why accept that life involves commitments, with all their necessary choices and forfeits?

Both responses are possible. Both exist in this world of ours. But I would say that the option for eternal youth, or something that looks like it, is gaining more followers right now. Currently, in our culture, the features of Peter Pan, the boy who refused to grow up, have become widespread. Maybe with a bit more depth of character than the boy in the book or films, but with the same fear of the decisive step into adulthood.

Peter Pan is the main character in the play, and subsequent book, *Peter Pan or The Boy Who Wouldn't Grow Up / Peter Pan and Wendy* by

J. M. Barrie, originally published in 1904, and frequently revisited by popular culture. He became a Disney hero, fighting Captain Hook in *Peter Pan*. He became the father of a family and a successful lawyer who has to re-learn how to have fun instead of being boring and stressed out in Steven Spielberg's film *Hook*. In the romance *Finding Neverland*, Johnny Depp is the writer J. M. Barrie who invents Peter Pan and an imaginary country to help the family next door escape from the difficulties of everyday life. Something that all three film versions have in common is that the character of Peter Pan is toned down and sweetened, becoming heroic, simple and attractive. In the original play and book Peter Pan is a selfish, problematic character who has opted to avoid the responsibilities of adult life because he doesn't want to grow up.

Psychologists today talk about 'Peter Pan syndrome', meaning reluctance to take on the complications, commitments and hard graft of adult life. This may be because of fear, insecurity, selfishness, an inability to do without certain inessentials, or dislike of responsibilities, or even because the person cannot find an opening to make their way into adult life. Whatever the reason, the temptation to take refuge in Neverland is evident.

These days you constantly hear references to eternal youth. It's a call, almost a command, to stay young, to feel young forever. The reverse side of this is a demonisation of anything connected with being adult or being older. Feeling old is even perceived as being in bad taste. In my view, it's just as problematic to try and stretch out your youth, not allowing yourself to grow up, as it is to pretend to be an adult before you really are one. Each stage in life has its own beauty, at the right time.

I remember clearly the day I turned forty. I got plenty of birthday greetings and messages. Quite a number of them, after the usual 'Happy Birthday' and 'Best Wishes' bits, added words of encouragement, sympathy or actual condolence. Plenty of people seemed to take it for granted that entering on this new decade was necessarily traumatic, and they tried to soften the shock for me with sympathetic and jokey messages, all variations on the standard war-cry 'Cheer up! Forty is the new twenty!'

'Who would want to be twenty again?!' I thought to myself. No way would I ever want to go through that stage a second time. The inner turmoil, the insecurity of not yet knowing how many experiences were awaiting you, or what they were ... It's true that there were also marvellous things, and maybe you do sometimes feel nostalgic for aspects of those times. The strength and vitality, the intensity of feelings, growing friendships, good health at that time when you didn't even know what backache was, knowing that there still lay ahead so many significant landmarks to achieve, so many stages to travel through, so many steps that now lie long in the past. Yes, of course it's fine to be young.

The mistake is to want to hold on to that youthfulness. Let's think of one aspect, looking after yourself. I think that the world of aesthetics, personal beauty, is a good pointer to what is happening. What strikes you is all the things that revolve around the pursuit of youthfulness and freshness: creams, treatments, operations, exercise programmes ... As we know, more and more people, at a progressively earlier age, are going in for cosmetic surgery. Avoiding wrinkles, reducing fat, removing bags under the eyes, remodelling the body, changing facial features to match certain standards ... And the whole time, maintaining youthful freshness and tautness is one of the most desirable goals of all.

Let's imagine for a moment that all those surgical procedures went well. Let's try and forget the mess-ups we've seen in some people who wanted to preserve or restore their former beauty and found their faces had been turned into grotesque masks instead. Even if everyone were able to keep their youthful smoothness and bloom, what would the world be like if you couldn't tell the differences between the parents' generation and the children's? That universal sameness would be scary. We would have lost the specific beauty of adult beings. The beauty of the passing of time, and the marks it leaves. Because faces tell a story. They speak of care, laughter, battles, tiredness. These marks of the passage of time have their own beauty.

The obsession persists. Some years ago a Spanish national newspaper published an article in its weekend edition under the title 'The secret of eternal youth'. The introductory paragraph ran, 'We spend hundreds of euros on creams and treatments to keep a younger-looking skin, cover up wrinkles or make them disappear. But the real secret lies in what we eat.' And what it recommended was watermelon, tomatoes, kiwis, pomegranates, marrows, spinach, red peppers, broccoli, avocados and strawberries. Apart from the fact that this diet doesn't hold much appeal for carnivores like me, what struck me at that point was the title, with its invitation to pursue and obtain eternal youth. Obviously it was not meant to be taken literally, and the article included the ideas of self-care and healthy aging, but it seemed to me to be a good journalistic reflection of a widespread ambition. Holding on hungrily to youth, youthfulness, the springtime of life, was the passion felt by Dorian Gray, and he paid for it with his soul.

Exactly the same can happen on the existential level. What has been said above about the obsession with eternal physical youth is intended as an introduction to something deeper. The longing for youth that many people feel today has a lot to do with the fact that they don't know about, or forget, the beauty and meaning of adult life, like Peter Pan, who was so determined to take refuge in Neverland. But when they try to freeze-frame the dance with time, what do they lose out on?

You don't grow up in a day

Years ago, I had a running joke with a young man in the pastoral centre where I worked. At that stage, like many others, he was a lad who played different roles depending on which aspect of life he found himself in at that moment. He was a good student. He was a believer, seeking for more, and pleasure-loving in his free time, sometimes excessively so. Nothing unusual for his age. His college years were going by, and from the time when he hit twenty onwards, I often used to ask him, 'When are you going to settle down?' And he invariably answered, 'When I'm twenty-seven.' Needless to say, more years went by, and he showed not the slightest sign of settling down to anything. His twenty-seventh birthday arrived, and I wasted no time in sending him a WhatsApp asking if the time had come. Right at the end of the day, I got a caustic message in reply, accompanied by an emoticon: 'When I'm thirty-five.'

I remember the episode with a smile, but it makes me think of a very basic fact: you don't grow up from one day to the next. The journey of leaving Peter Pan behind is in fact a long one, offering more than one battle to fight, and it passes through little victories in which you need to begin cultivating some aspects of adult life.

I lived in a hall of residence for university students for fifteen years. It was surprising to see how often, when there had been some conflict and disciplinary measures had to be applied, the parents of the student concerned turned up, to try and get their son out of trouble. They used all sorts of arguments, but there was one that invariably appeared: 'Don't hold it against him. Can't you see he's still just a child?' I really felt like shaking these parents and telling them that their son was not a child any more; he was a young man, old enough to drive, vote, drink and also go to prison. It was wrong to want to deprive their sons of the lessons you learn when you face up to the consequences of your own decisions, including your mistakes. Don't get me wrong, I'm not talking about any crushing punishments, expulsion from the university or a public hanging. I'm talking about things like imposing a curfew, spending a weekend indoors, doing a day of reflection, and maybe, at most, being asked to leave the hall of residence. Nothing that would cause any great trauma. In education, disciplinary measures have a clear goal. Being able to take such steps, impose sanctions, is a way of teaching students that there are limits in life, which is undeniable, whether we like it or not. And there are limits when we live with others.

Little by little you have to learn to take your own decisions and face up to the consequences of your choices. You have to swallow the small doses of responsibility that accompany your steps forward, the choices you make and their results.

When you're little you normally have the safety net of parents who protect you. They cushion any blows, put you straight and watch your steps for you. But as life proceeds that safety net disappears. Adults are required to be responsible. And as I said earlier, that doesn't just happen between one day and the next. You can't be irresponsible until you're twenty-six and then suddenly become perfectly responsible on your twenty-seventh birthday. Life isn't like that.

Unfortunately, today we meet huge numbers of Peter Pans as far as taking responsibility goes. Perhaps it's because they've never been able, or been taught, to develop responsibility as a virtue. They are eternally irresponsible, always blaming others for anything that goes wrong.

Who is able, these days, to admit their mistakes publicly? When someone actually does, it's so unusual it even sparks applause. Which politician, for example, is able to admit that the undesirable consequences of a badly thought-out law require them to at least own up to their mistake? It's always easier to blame everyone else, or circumstances, or simply refuse to recognise the unwelcome fact. Peter Pan is alive and well.

Choosing and renouncing: two sides of a coin

It takes time to grow from a young person into an adult. You learn little by little. The first decisions are plagued by adolescent doubts, which seem endless once you get to that stage. Your first friends, the first things you buy unsupervised, a way of dressing that shows the image you want to project, the first trip you make without your parents, your first dabblings in love … Later you'll have more serious decisions to take. Shall I go to college or get a job? What subject shall I take? Shall I start on a serious relationship? Shall I leave home? Shall I risk going abroad for a time to earn my living? Along the way you have to learn how to live with rules you don't always like. Sometimes you get things wrong. Getting everything right one hundred per cent of the time is an impossible dream. There are no guarantees. To complicate things still further, when you choose one path, you have to turn your back on other paths. That may be the hardest thing about making decisions: everything that involves saying no to other possibilities. Because choosing also means relinquishing, and that is totally counter-cultural in today's world.

Young people are told: You can experience everything. Try everything. Why should you give up anything? Why close any doors, if you can live with all of them open? Travel all over the world. Experience everything.

Try out all the lives there are. How can you know that you don't like something if you haven't tried it?

We're supposed to be in an age of infinite possibilities. It's about building a life where frustration and disappointment don't happen, even in the slightest degree. Desire is king.

Of course, you may be forced to mature due to a traumatic experience, or you may discover the hard way that the dream of having everything forever was a pipe dream. Ideally, this learning process would be progressive over time, from childhood onwards. However, today it seems that too often the over-protection of children is giving them a real inability to deal with any disappointment or failure.

Nowadays, everything that sounds like disappointment, resignation or limits has a very bad press. The imperative of personal well-being has gradually acquired citizenship status. Your world, your rules! Reality will be what you want it to be. If anything bothers you, you have the right to make it disappear. Political correctness is gaining ground in language. The culture of cancelling everything (or everyone) you don't agree with and eliminating the possibility of failure – which, as I've already pointed out, we see happening in schools – all of this is a strange sign of the softness of a society that wants to keep its subjects in cotton wool, in a deceitful illusion of comfort.

That's the drama of Peter Pan. Refusing to face the uncertainties, griefs and renunciations of adult life. Continuing for as long as you can to move within a safe, familiar sphere, where you enjoy the relative autonomy of someone who is no longer a child, but where you have not yet had to close too many doors.

Whose fault is it?

I know this chapter looks like being heavy on young people. I want to emphasise something I've already said. This is not their fault. In fact, many young people don't have the Peter Pan attitude or want it. They want to grow up, and, if many of them can't do so faster, it's not for lack of will but lack of opportunities. To a large extent, if anyone is to blame, it's the many adults who have created the breeding ground for this whole situation.

It could be argued that our society seems not to favour young people growing up early. Very often, they can't become independent and can't find stable jobs. Even those who do work, can't afford a home of their own. If bringing children into the world is increasingly a luxury ... and if it's difficult to create the conditions that would truly allow adult life from an early age ... then perhaps it's more convenient to discourage dreams, limit horizons, operate in the short term, prolong the age of possibilities, replace vital choices with constant consumerism and delay the moment of stepping into adult life for as long as possible. The only thing that lets us down here is the biological clock, which does not allow motherhood to be postponed beyond a certain age. But even that is beginning to be managed.

If that were all, we might conclude that in our society becoming an adult is seen as something desirable, but the conditions do not allow it. The reality, as I believe I have already shown, is that many *adults* would prefer not to be adults. It is adults, not young people, who suffer from the Peter Pan complex. Young people are living through what they should be living through at their age: turbulence, multiple choices, searches, insecurities, fleetingness, the intensity of strong opinions above all ... The problem is that many adults continue playing the same game, when they should have left all of that behind. There are many adults who try to convince themselves, as I said earlier, that forty is the new twenty. They are always going on about how 'I still feel young.' They vaunt their decision to skim over the realities of life without ever putting down roots in anything. They argue, out of a questionable rebelliousness, that the only criterion of truth and reality is one's own self. They sceptically deny the possibility of a love that will last forever; they want no limits or restrictions; they have a ready-made speech about how you shouldn't deny yourself a single whim, since after all, life is so brief. And I won't even mention those who manage their midlife crises badly, thinking that by behaving and dressing like teenagers or surrounding themselves with people who are half their age, they will turn back the clock.

The only thing that is achieved by people who choose this approach, who pretend to be young, is that they treat real young people like adolescents. They don't let them travel along the paths I was talking about before: responsibility, assuming the consequences of their own actions and accepting the need for renunciation.

Even worse is what these Peter Pans miss. In their daydream of eternal youth, in their mythification of the age of possibilities, they fail to perceive the beauty of moving forward in life, consolidating projects, taking root and seeing the fruits. The issue of mid-life crises and the inability to grow has been discussed in many ways and formats. A few years ago the neologism 'adultescent' became popular, which sums up the whole description of an adult who behaves like a selfish, egocentric young person.

Once again, cinema captures this well. The Italian film *L'Ultimo Bacio*, 'The Last Kiss', is an amusing reflection on the fear of moving on. Carlo is about to marry Giulia, his pregnant girlfriend. When he crosses paths with the young girl Francesca, he finds himself having to choose between settling down and starting his own family or going back to the carefree light-heartedness of youth. Of course, at this crossroads he makes a big mistake, fantasising about a new, youthful love affair. It is refreshing – from the outside – to see his absurd, endearing and at the same time pathetic attempts to cling on to a bygone stage in his life. The contrast between the adolescent Francesca and the adult Giulia is also thought provoking. And Carlo is not the only one who experiences this dilemma. Almost all the characters in this coming-of-age story, his lifelong friends, are going through their own crises: Alberto, who lives from one flirtation to another without being able to forge any real relationships; Paolo, depressed by his father's illness; and Adriano, whose marriage is in crisis.

Some characters will mature. Others will end up choosing the path of eternal adolescence. The director seems to come down on the side of maturity, although, with a certain final cynicism, he leaves open the possibility of always continuing to look back.

What will you feel, as the viewer? Pity for these eternal adolescents, who are incapable of maturing but remain trapped in the labyrinth of expectations or scepticism about the apparent solidity of adult life?

Learning to love the grey days

Young people, don't be fooled by Peter Pan. Don't be seduced by the chimera of a 'lite' life, without ties and without roots. Don't buy into the deceptive discourse that seems determined to freeze life's flow at just one stage. Enjoy youth in all its beauty, fight for its lessons of growth, celebrate it in its joyful learning processes and in its fleeting light-heartedness, but don't mythologise it to the point of wanting to eternalise it, because you will be missing out on the beauty, the passion and the depth of what comes next.

Being an adult is not boring; it's not passively accepting the grey days. It's about learning to value them as much as the special ones and discovering the enormous range of their tones.

There are many people who think that the best life is one that consists of a never-ending series of intense, exciting, unique moments. That success has to be immediate. That results are obtained just by wanting them ... When you see the world like that, the everyday seems a bit scary. Everything that is boring seems like a failure. The long term seems like a prison sentence. Everything has to be special, unique, novel, imaginative, creative, different ... Well, if I could keep just one thing from the learning process at this stage of life, it would be: learn to love the 'grey days'. Learn to enjoy the daily rhythm. Learn to find the value of ordinary life. Because that is precisely what will make some moments extraordinary. Learn the value of a commitment that, although it starts from great intuitions, is later built up on quiet deeds, on many moments that will not leave much of a mark, and on discreet and often hidden work. Because that commitment is what will give meaning to the important things in your life: the passion that materialises in a vocation, the relationships on which you want to build a family and a story, the faith that enables you to believe in human beings, in justice, in the possibilities of society or in God.

If someone tells you that every moment in life ought to be special, unique and outstanding, don't believe them; they're either lying or mistaken. What will give some moments their special character is building them on a life rooted in people, places and daily commitments.

True adult life is watering what you have sown, watching it grow slowly and having the patience to wait for it to bear fruit. It's about understanding that love has subtleties that you never imagined. It means discovering that the enormous lessons that life offers you in the years of your youth are followed by other more delicate ones that are richer in nuances, perhaps less showy, but that give your story serenity, depth and an unsuspected, unimagined range of colours. True adult life means understanding that commitments are not chains but connections, and that they don't tie you down to life and people but rather keep you united, like the anchor that has to be cast at some point in life.

5

Dancing with Time:
beyond *Carpe Diem*

Have you seen the film *Dead Poets Society*? I'm one of the people who wept when John Keating's class in the Welton Academy stood up on their desks calling, 'O Captain! My Captain!' I too had been seduced by his transgressive teaching, his provocative cry, his rejection of oppressive traditions and his invitation to take risks in the present without postponing everything until a future that might never come. '*Carpe diem!*' he taught those apprentice poets, quoting the end of 'Ode 1.11' by the Roman poet Horace, who ends his reflection on the brevity of life with the disturbing words, 'Seize the day and do not trust tomorrow.'

It took me years to spot the hidden trap in the sentimental wrapping of the film. I'm not ashamed to say that I liked it then, and I still like it now. I think that, properly understood, its thesis of facing the present moment is valuable, necessary and very applicable in some areas of life. It could be a warning against dilettantes, who by postponing decisions will never decide anything.

There is a much more superficial interpretation of *carpe diem*, and this is the one that has really prevailed in our unstable culture. It exalts the present at the cost of ignoring the past and refusing to look to the future. Yesterday is gone, we don't know if tomorrow will come, so let's live in the here and now, with no memory and no plans. Now is what we have. Today is what matters. A few years ago, a Spanish mobile-phone advertisement aimed at young consumers tried to turn *carpe diem* into a slogan for an entire generation: 'Be a *nower*'.[4] The message was very direct:

---

4. https://www.youtube.com/watch?v=Vtj8BRUCbEI.

They said, '*carpe diem*', and you took it to extremes! You're not content to enjoy the moment, you want to capture it! Live every moment as if it were the last! Make it eternal, relive everything that makes you feel awake! Travel to the ends of the earth! Learn five languages! Taste all the delights hidden in every corner! Your life is now! And this is where we come in – a generation that wants to squeeze out life to the very utmost! We don't just want to enjoy the moment, we want to capture it! We want to live every moment to the limit, and make it eternal! Capture now! Be a *nower*!

Like anything to do with advertising, it shouldn't be taken out of context. As an ad for mobile phones it grabs attention very effectively. The way it plays with the idea of capturing life (in images) with a good built-in camera is likewise very effective. But latent in the script, behind its fun presentation, is a whole concept of life that if you take it seriously, will cheat you.

Carpe diem!

Carpe diem means literally 'seize the day' or in other words, 'Live in the now'; *now* is the time that matters. As I have already pointed out, there are many ways of understanding this phrase. It could be a way of not escaping into daydreams about the future or not getting stuck in the mazes of the past. In that sense it has a point. But it could also be a way of reducing time to the present moment, and that's a risky bet that ends up going wrong.

OK, there is a stage in life when *carpe diem* carries more weight. When *now* is an urgent call for action. Youth is a time when it makes sense. Back in the sixteenth century, the Spanish poet Garcilaso de la Vega invited young people to 'gather the sweet fruit of your joyful spring, before time's stormy weather covers the fair peaks with snow' (Sonnet 23). Yes, there are stages when you need a certain lightness, a good dose of celebration, making the most of the freedom given by not yet having any roots, when tiredness is easily overcome with a few hours of sleep.

In youth, the past is still too close for you to read it in perspective, yet as an adolescent you spend years trying to leave behind the child you were. You desire to grow up, to establish areas of autonomy and no longer be treated like a child. As an adolescent you're often embarrassed when adults insist on describing episodes from your childhood to other adults. Everything that seems to anchor you to your childhood annoys you. The past has not yet become a treasure, or a school, or a place to return to in order to retrieve so many episodes that you don't yet know how to value.

You're facing forward, towards the enormous potential you want to realise: autonomy, freedom, fun, a sense of independence, your own path, responsibility ...

These days, though, however much young people want to look ahead, the future makes many of them feel dizzy. Thinking about something stable, established, a long-term project, involves so many uncertainties that you can't look at it seriously without feeling overwhelmed. You can't be sure you'll find a permanent job. Or to find work you may have to emigrate to another country, and you are not sure if you'd want to stay there for life. Maybe owning a home seems to be within reach only of the most privileged. Maybe starting a family sounds frightening, both with regard to money and in terms of your personal life. There is increasing scepticism about long-term relationships in this world of short emotional cycles, where endings and new beginnings happen one after the other, and none of them leave much of a mark. If these and other considerations all converge ... it is understandable when young people opt for a permanently short-term outlook.

Perhaps you don't indulge in an absolute present, just a fairly wide present, where plans don't go too far ahead so as not to have to deal with frustrations later.

So you don't look much to the past because it's already behind you, and the future or the long term seems too far away. In the end the big bet is on what is immediate, on the present, the here and now.

The problem is that living in an absolute present, excluding the past and the future, would be as bad as an absolute past or an absolute future. It's good to look to the past, because it can be a school, because it's part of the truth of our own life, and because there are experiences in it that no one can take away from us, but trying to remain in a happy past means giving up on living. Valuing the past is good, as long as it doesn't become a prison. What's more, looking to the future is something we need to do, but if it's so invasive, so demanding or so utopian that there's no way to live with it peacefully, then it can become a prison that is just as dark as the prison of nostalgia.

A dance in three tempos

Becoming an adult is about learning to dance with time, and dancing with time doesn't mean falling into a blinkered, absolute present, nor into the prison of the past, nor into the escapism of the future. Dancing with time means taking ownership of our own life story. Understanding that on our life path, what we have lived through in the past converges with and intertwines with our present and with our expectations for the future. Past, present and future are woven together to make us into people with a story. Adults are people who are aware of their own story, which is a work in progress. A story that will have to be lived in three tempos. A dance that will combine three intertwined melodies in a single soundtrack, the soundtrack of life itself.

Valuing the past

Perhaps it's normal for young people to look more to the present or the future than back. Partly because they're in a hurry to push the limits of their own autonomy, and partly because they don't yet feel they have much of a past. Psychologists insist that our first years have a strong influence on who we will be throughout the rest of our lives, and undoubtedly adolescents and young people, just like adults, are conditioned by those early steps, but it takes time to become aware of this.

Perhaps what you lack, when you are young, is enough distance to be able to treasure your past. Your lived experience is in reality an enormously rich resource that can enable you to journey ahead through life with firm steps. I think the Spanish writer Javier Aznar expresses it perfectly.

> In certain moments of confusion when we don't know which
> direction to take, and are moving forward with a troubled,
> broken soul, we need to look back, very far back, to under-
> stand who we are and where we're going. Press the rewind
> key, see our life from the opposite direction, stop at a cer-
> tain point that maybe we didn't notice at the time but which
> from the perspective of the present, is like a revelation flash
> that explains much of what we are.[5]

Yesterday is an indispensable ally in our inner battles. There are three
reasons for this. First, because in it we are carrying a lot of luggage –
think equipment – that will always be with us. Secondly, because it's a
school and a source of wisdom if we know how to read it properly. And
thirdly, because it's also a place to return to for rest.

When I say that our past holds very valuable luggage, what I mean is
that what we have lived through is part of what we are today. If the only
real thing were the here and now, we would always be at the mercy of
circumstances. We would be like weather-vanes, forced to move whatever
way the wind blows. An absolute present would make us totally dependent on fashions, on our current feelings or on changing circumstances.

Our lives hold an enormous wealth of names, stories and moments
that are part of who we are today. This is especially clear when we think
of the people, the names from our past who no longer figure in our everyday lives. Obviously not everyone who's ever been important to you is
present with you today. Rarely could anyone keep open all the connections and channels of communication in their life.

There are so many ways in which once-convergent paths become sepa-
rate. It may be death, which sometimes takes away those we love, often
leaving a huge void. It may be conflict, which makes those who once
walked together unable to continue. And almost always it's life circumstances that introduce distances between people: moving to another
town, undertaking new projects. Lives change and new commitments
come to the fore.

5.   Javier Aznar, *¿Dónde vamos a bailar esta noche?* (Madrid: Círculo de Tiza, 2017), p. 67.

And it's not just people but many other reflections from the past: things, places, experiences, first times, steps that can only be taken once in a lifetime, news, events that you witnessed whether in society or in your own story.

All that has happened is not just left behind in the past; it doesn't just get lost. It's part of your present. It's there in your memory. It's there in the traces it has left in you. What built you up in the past is still there in the strength you have today. You carry with you the hugs received. Likewise the blows, and the way you learned to face them. You carry the songs that were once the soundtrack for your life. You carry the places where you were happy. The routines that came to constitute your small story. Your favourite films, which touched chords that went beyond what appeared on the screen. The battles you once fought. You carry it all because it is part of you.

For example, death doesn't take away your love. It doesn't even take away the people you love. They remain in your memory. What you experienced with them is part of who you are now. For as long as some words remain in your memory, they remain, in some way, alive in you.

The second reason for respecting the past is that it is a school. 'Experience' means being able to read clearly what we have lived through. When we talk about having experience of something, what we mean is that we have lived it, gone through it, and learned something as a result. Think about work. If someone is looking for people with experience in a field, it means people who have learned, in previous situations, what is involved in that field of work. Well, life is a constant collection of experience. We can learn from both successes and mistakes. And this is true in many areas of life. We get to know the world we are part of, what people are like, or the dynamics of our society. We get to know ourselves. Our experiences mark us. We learn that people react differently in similar situations. And we need to learn how we ourselves react. We learn to love and to hate, to dance, to believe, to pray, to suspect. We learn to fall and get up again. We learn to set ourselves goals and attain some of them, and fail at others. To tell the truth, and to lie. We draw conclusions from everything we experience.

They say that the human being is the only animal that trips on the same stone twice, maybe not just twice but many more times. Human beings are also capable of learning to avoid the stones that hurt us. That's what looking back is about.

The third reason for looking at the past is that it's somewhere it can be pleasant to return to. Of course we can choose to forget some experiences or lock away some difficult episodes in rooms we don't wish to walk through, but it is a privilege to be able to return to experiences, moments, episodes that we know are part of our lives. Adults tend to do this a lot; they are already far enough away from their past, from their childhood and youth, to begin to enjoy these return trips.

So part of the experience of the past when you're an adult is to learn to value all the luggage you carry. It means converting experience into a resource and a source of wisdom and giving yourself permission to return, occasionally, to the places where you grew up, but you have to know how to do it. Don't let that look at the past turn into a prison cell. That will happen if you fall into the trap of nostalgia and let it become a labyrinth.

The past is luggage that you carry with you, but it isn't all of your luggage. Experience is a source of wisdom, but it shouldn't become the inexorable sentence that everything must always be done in the same way as before, 'because it's always been that way'. The past is a place to go back to, not to stay in, but to return to the present from. It's good to travel to the past, to evoke and visit places, times and ages. However, there is the danger of getting trapped by some episodes, whether beautiful or tragic (there are all kinds). Sometimes a memory wants to bury us in a cell with the ghost of those we once loved, before something went wrong. Or we see, over and over again, choices we shouldn't have made or blows that knocked us down, and then regret, anguish or reproach grip our hearts. Sometimes we return incessantly to a particular experience that marked us, wanting to relive it, although we know we can't.

The memory of the past becomes a labyrinth when, instead of being a grateful, evocative resource, it becomes an obstacle to going forward.

A few years ago the film *Manchester by the Sea* was very popular. The story it tells is a tragic one. Lee Chandler is a surly, distant man who leads a dull existence as a plumber, doing odd jobs in Boston, fighting in seedy bars and living poorly in a hovel. When he returns to his hometown, Manchester, after his brother dies, he has to face the past. Over the course of a few terrible days, we learn about Lee's tragedy. A fire, caused by his carelessness, killed his three small children. Since then, Lee has been unable to turn the page. There is no forgiveness possible for him, nor any new beginning. He has chosen to live in the prison of the past and punish himself mercilessly for what happened. A conversation with his ex-wife and mother of his children gives the key to this choice. She tells him that he has to forgive himself and move on, that no matter how broken they both are, life goes on, but he is absolutely incapable of doing so. He is someone trapped in a past that has swallowed up everything.

Obviously, that particular film is about an exceptionally traumatic situation, and probably none of us would be capable of dealing with a tragedy like that, but it does show how past events can become a cage, and looking back on them is like a black hole we can't escape from.

What could someone do to get out of such a labyrinth? There are four attitudes, all equally necessary: accept, be grateful, learn, and move on.

Maybe the hardest but also most necessary one is to accept. Accept that we can't change the past, and that we can't hold on to it. It's not that we can lose it – it's part of our luggage. But we need to learn how to put it in the right place. It's just as important to accept the bad parts as to treasure the good parts. It's fundamental to learn how to be grateful for what was good and beautiful in the past, and just as fundamental to recognise our defeats and mistakes and to learn from successes and failures alike, from the things we got wrong just as much as from the things we got right. What we should never stop doing is looking to the future. It's not about forgetting anything – it would be stupid to want to do that. It's about refusing to let ourselves be imprisoned by our memories. Life goes on. Desires, plans, names, stories – all of them point us to the future. There are paths to be taken, a life to be lived, outside the labyrinths of the past.

On the temptation to change the past, a very interesting approach was the one in the book *Atonement,* by Ian McEwan, and the 2007 film made from the book. In the 1930s, Briony is a young girl who, suffering from adolescent jealousy, ruins the lives of her older sister Cecilia and Cecilia's boyfriend Robbie by accusing him of rape. The novel follows the stories of these characters. Cecilia and Robbie manage to meet again after the Second World War, and finally recover some of the happiness that has been denied them. Lovely ... but untrue. In reality Cecilia was killed in the Blitz and Robbie during the evacuation from Dunkirk. The happy ending was just a story within the story, written by Briony, now grown up, repentant and a novelist. She justifies it by asking why she should write about a depressing past instead of offering her (fictional) readers an alternative world, but for us, the real readers, the revelation of her lie, this discovery of the final tragedy, this story with no redemption, comes as a final blow. But it's the truth, and there is nothing to be gained by sweetening it if we want to know the true story. Respecting the past means not wanting to rewrite it.

I'll finish this section about the past with a story I found both fascinating and disturbing. Once again, film becomes a source of questions, of dilemmas. This time it is the film *Reminiscence*. In a post-apocalyptic world, Miami is flooded as a result of climate change. Nick Bannister is a private investigator who enables clients to recover their lost memories. By entering an immersive tank, 'the reminiscence', they can relive events in the past with total clarity. This memory machine can be used to find lost objects, solve murders, or relive times when the subject was happy.

Nick himself embarks on a maddening search where he has to try and find Mae, a beautiful woman he fell in love with during an investigation. They had a relationship as intense as it was mysterious, but then she vanished without a trace. Spoiler alert: when Nick reaches the end of his investigation, he will discover that Mae is dead. He is faced with a crossroads. He can move on, because life goes on. However, he chooses to spend the rest of his life in a dream tank, reliving his love story over and over again.

Reminiscence poses a key question. Is this loop of remembered happiness life? Is this chosen nostalgia an adult option, or is it actually the escapism of someone who is unable to accept the passage of time, with its limitations? Isn't Nick's choice a refusal to live, being imprisoned by what he wanted to hold on to? Respecting and valuing the past means being able to put it in its place.

Respecting the present

My criticism of certain ways of understanding *carpe diem* doesn't mean that the present doesn't matter. Of course it matters. Every part of time is necessary, so it doesn't make sense to take refuge in a happier past, or to turn the future into a dream to escape from the here and now. Of course you sometimes have to sacrifice part of the present for future achievements, but do so without forgetting to make the most of your life here and now, at every moment.

One of the articles in the series on advice to the younger self, cited in chapter 2, gives a very interesting key to understanding. A computer engineer, the thirty-year-old father of a family, looks at his younger self and advises him to do a different, and necessary, *carpe diem*. This is his reflection, which comes in very aptly here.

> My name is Juan Carlos, thirty, I'm a son, father, husband and computer engineer. I work in digital communication.
>
> Juan (I would tell my younger self), you're now twenty, and I know you feel a bit lost. I know you're putting pressure on yourself to be 'a worthwhile person'. But what exactly does that mean? To you, at this crossroads, knowing everything that you're going to experience, I would say: live in the moment. I don't mean party all the time; I know you'd like to, but that will pass. Living in the moment means much more.
>
> I mean that when you're studying, do it with passion because you realise that this time is a privilege, and you'll even come to like it. When it's time for fun, live it intensely – one day you'll need those memories, and long for those times when you shared a beer. When you have a hard time, don't try to bury it. Those are the times I've learned the most

from. Hiding them (even from yourself) does you no good. Live through the boring times and let your imagination fly. They're not a waste of time, believe me. Don't stop talking to God, and dedicate time to him in your everyday doings, even if it's sometimes difficult. It will serve as a guide, a consolation, a joy, and it will give you a sense of the truest peace there is ... Take time to relax, and get enough sleep, because without that you won't be able to live through the rest of your time intensely. I repeat, none of this is a waste of time.

Living in the present moment doesn't mean planning what will come next and trying to have everything under control. That can be good in a way, but you also have to live now, feel, let yourself go and leave space for surprises.

Be careful not to rush too much. My ambition to reach the goals I set for myself year after year has made me rush through stages, perhaps too quickly. Don't fall into that, because if at twenty-five you live like someone who's thirty, no matter how proud you feel, you will miss having been twenty-five, with all the lessons that were there for you. And twenty, twenty-one, twenty-two or twenty-five will not come back. Don't rush through stages of your life. Go slowly.

Everything has its time. Everything comes, but everything also passes. Live in it.[6]

There is some much-needed wisdom in this reflection. Perhaps it is the same wisdom that led the author of the Book of Ecclesiastes to write, in chapter 3, one of the best-known passages on time, where he points out that there is a time for everything (Eccles 3:1–8). He spoke of things that mattered then and also now: being born, dying, uprooting, harvesting, speaking, keeping silent, destroying, building, weeping, laughing ... Probably we'd put in some different things today, but the message is the same. There is a time for everything: for solitude and

6. J. C. Manso, 'Live in the present moment, leave space for surprises, and don't rush', pastoralsj .org, https://pastoralsj.org/ser/1889-de-vivir-el-momento-dejar-espacio-a-la-sorpresa-y-nocorrer -demasiado.

for meeting people, for believing and for doubting, for seeking and for leaving aside, for reading, watching films, working, studying, going out, dancing, cooking and eating; for planning and for improvising. There is a time for drawing, a time for chats, a time for praying, reading, going for walks, travelling, loving ...

Maybe one of the lessons that comes with life, and one that needs to be taken on board and integrated into the life of every adult, is that respecting the present means making room in it for all life's various dimensions. Rejecting all enjoyment of the present for the sake of imaginary future triumphs would be as big a mistake as doing nothing but partying.

The fact that there is a time for everything, or that all these aspects of life have their place, doesn't mean that everything fits in at the same time. Perhaps learning to discern when is the right time for each thing is just as necessary as making space for all these different activities, working out when is the right time for solitude, and when is the time for getting together with people; when is the right time for words, and when it's best to keep silent.

What I'm trying to explain can be summed up in one word: balance. We need to get to a stage where we allow space and time for the various aspects of human life. Obviously that balance won't be the same for everyone; it depends on our personal circumstances, likes and dislikes, and character. Everyone's life can't be divided up into identical sections, because lives are different, circumstances are different and people are different too. Some people go crazy if they have to keep still for too long, while others need a slower pace. But having said that, what everyone needs to learn one way or another is how to respect the present. And what does that respect consist of? Respecting the present means accepting difficult times when they come, without being overwhelmed by the darkness, setbacks or pain they may involve. One of the most surprising dynamics in our time is that as soon as someone feels bad, it is absolutely imperative for them to recover their well-being. It's understandable; everyone wants to be well and happy. Nobody wants to have a bad time, but that can't be a condition for continuing to live, because the reality is that circumstances will often have you on the ropes. Sometimes the wounds inflicted by an event, a relationship, a frustrated project, whatever, will make you cry, and the wounds of that story can take time to heal. Covering that up by taking refuge in a joy that doesn't really exist is like trying to cheat life, and such tricks don't work.

Respecting the present means knowing how to enjoy times of happiness, giving yourself permission, sometimes, to waste time, because the whole of your life can't be totally useful, fruitful and productive. It means finding spaces in everyday life to share a good time with someone, a light-hearted chat about trivialities, a walk, or simply switching off from work.

Respecting the present means dealing with conflicts when they arise. One of the greatest difficulties for many people is not knowing how to face up to unpleasant situations. The temptation is always to put off uncomfortable conversations until later, to let time pass, to see if knots straighten themselves out, to leave for later steps that should be taken now. That was precisely what Keating, the teacher in *Dead Poets Society*, meant by *carpe diem*. If you postpone problems you ought to face now, you'll always find excuses for yet another postponement. This doesn't mean that it's never right to postpone certain decisions, efforts or actions, but habitually avoiding difficulties is harmful.

Respecting the present means making an effort to find out about the world you live in. I'm often surprised by the way misinformation – deliberate ignorance – is gaining ground. How many people choose not to know. With the world in such bad shape, with the endless noise produced by social networks, with the difficulty in making sense of current problems, and with the number of biases driving the media, it's not surprising that many people prefer to take refuge in a bubble and reduce the world to '*my* world'. But the reality is that knowing the society in which you live, this globally interconnected world, human dynamics, advances, technology, economic interests, the great debates of our time and what they are based on – all of this provides perspective, depth and realism. Many of our personal mini-dramas simply melt away once we see them from the perspective of the wider world.

Respecting the present means shouldering the amount of routine, day-to-day living and habit that there is in every life. If you want to live permanently on an emotional rollercoaster, you'll be lost. If you try to turn your life into an endless pursuit of unique, special moments and intense emotions, not only will you find it impossible, but you'll also fail to recognise the real beauty of everyday life, the strength that grows from habits and routines, the ability to perceive nuances in apparently interchangeable days.

Respecting the present means knowing how to slow down from time to time to take the pulse of life, because otherwise it can happen that you end up becoming an automaton, trapped in inertia or incapable of understanding the things that happen to you. You need to stop to examine your life, to dare to ask yourself occasionally, 'What's going on, where am I heading, what's happening to me?' To learn to describe your feelings and current concerns, to identify your underlying motivations, the things that keep you awake and on track.

Respecting the present means, finally, respecting the people who are part of that present. In every story there is, at any given moment, a cluster of relationships. Your present is not just you. It's also the people who, at each stage, love you, put up with you, are there for you; and the people you in your turn love, put up with and are there for – people you have real connections to through affection, work, community and family.

Today we live so fast that in fact we often miss out on other people's lives. We act like each of us is nothing more than another presence to be swiped up on a mobile phone. We go that easily from one face to another, from one life to another. So what does respecting these people mean? It means taking them seriously, caring for them and caring about them, not just turning them into a mirror where you can look at yourself according to your own moods, needs and concerns. It means having quality time for the important relationships in life. It means not taking people so much for granted that you ignore them, even if you don't actually forget them.

Looking to the future

One of the most deceitful things people can mean by the phrase *carpe diem* is 'don't think about tomorrow'. Since the future hasn't come yet, they argue, and we don't even know if it will, there's no point in worrying about it. This doesn't mean that they fail altogether to think or plan anything in life, but they usually make short-term plans, just enough to get by, and let the rest take care of itself.

Just as we noted earlier that young people don't yet have much of a past to go back to, it can happen that they don't have any clear future to look forward to. And hence the temptation of choosing to anchor themselves strictly in the present.

There could be many reasons for this choice. It's not just foolishness. The speed of change today is so dizzying; you may sometimes think it would be better to cling to the here and now, given how unforeseeable the shape of your life looks. The future is so uncertain that it may seem quite sensible to refuse to look that way in case you despair.

Thinking about the young people around today, uncertainty about the future is clear. It's highly unusual to find any kind of stability at least in the first few years of your working life. It's hard to settle anywhere when house prices are out of reach, and in many cases you can't even afford to move out of your parents' place. The idea of starting a family is enough to make you dizzy, involving so much commitment, expense and renunciation (the relative weight of each of these three elements will vary with the individual).

So of course you're tempted to delay looking at tomorrow for as long as you can. Most people know that at some point, they're going to have to look at the future, but more and more frequently they put off doing so out of a combination of prudence, resignation and irresponsibility.

Some years ago Baz Luhrmann, the director of films like *Moulin Rouge!*, the postmodern *Romeo + Juliet* and more recently the biopic *Elvis*, brought out a spoken-song video called 'Everybody's Free (To Wear Sunscreen)'.[7] It was based on a *Chicago Tribune* column by Mary Schmich and reflected on how pointless it is to give advice to young people.[8] Both article and video went viral.

---

7. 'Everybody's free to wear sunscreen', Baz Luhrmann, https://www.youtube.com/watch?v=5giWfpANMac.
8. Mary Schmich, 'Advice, Like Youth, Probably Just Wasted On The Young', *Chicago Tribune*, 1 June 1997.

What's interesting is to see how the advice offered in the column to young people included some seriously good ideas, together with others that were, to put it mildly, questionable. Two I found particularly striking were, 'Don't worry about the future; or worry, but know that worrying is as effective as trying to solve an algebra equation by chewing bubblegum. The real troubles in your life are apt to be things that never crossed your worried mind; the kind that blindside you at 4:00 pm on some idle Tuesday.' And: 'Don't feel guilty if you don't know what you wanna do with your life; the most interesting people I know didn't know at twenty-two what they wanted to do with their lives; some of the most interesting forty-year-olds I know still don't.'

Those phrases are eye-catching but somewhat superficial. Perhaps they contain something worthwhile. Sometimes the future is simply unpredictable; and sometimes the unexpected bursts out on you, shattering your previously-made plans, expectations and hopes. It's quite possible that when you're twenty, you don't know what you want to do with your life. But if you still don't know by the time you're forty, I suggest you need to think deeply about your attitude, because setting targets and thinking about tomorrow helps you move forward in the right direction. Also because life goes very fast – too fast to waste decades ambling around without taking the reins. Obviously I'm not talking about forcing yourself or stressing yourself out, but what you do need to do is set reference points in the future that draw you onwards today.

Any of us can look back at our life story and count a large number of paths in it that twisted, or straightened out, in ways we could never have foreseen.

It's true that you can't make rules about tomorrow, you can't control it, and that there is a good deal of uncertainty on all sides. The thesis that knowing the present could predict the future gave rise many years ago to one of the best-known science fiction series, Isaac Asimov's *Foundation* trilogy, now a popular television serial. There, a hypothetical social science, psychohistory, developed by Hari Seldon, enables the future to be predicted based on a knowledge of present trends. However, even in that universe, where the entire future had been studied, unexpected events could still upset what was predicted.

The mistake would be to conclude, because of this possible irruption of the unexpected, that it's better not to think about the future. Why make plans, you might argue, if the unexpected upsets them, smashes them, and on top of that you get upset for not having achieved what you wanted?

Looking to the future helps to complete the overall picture of time that we've been building up in this chapter on how time passes: valuing the past becomes a lesson and a source of wisdom, respecting the present means rejecting escapism and taking the here and now seriously, and the future pulls us forward towards our chosen target. Looking to the future provides us with three fundamental elements in life: it makes us responsible, it motivates us, and it offers us hope.

First of all, responsibility. Thinking about the future involves recognising that actions have consequences, and that although you can't control everything, what you can do is apply the means to achieve certain ends. It's important to learn long-term thinking. Decisions that seem unimportant, light, even trivial right now, may prove to be fruitful or sterile, healing or hurtful, productive or disastrous in the long term. As always, we learn from little things in order to apply the lesson to big things later on.

When you're young, one of the first battlefields is studying. 'Study now so that when the exams come, you won't be caught in a train wreck.' Everyone has heard these warnings. And probably many people learned through trial and error. You didn't study at the time, and you were caught in a train wreck. It wasn't an outright disaster. Failing that exam, or those exams, ended up being educational, a lesson for life. The encouraging note here is the idea of responsibility: taking responsibility for your decisions and the consequences they may have in the future. Today, when there's so much irresponsibility in so many spheres of life, honesty about your own choices is becoming more and more essential.

Next, motivation. Having future goals impels you to take steps in the present. The future can't be some kind of utopia disconnected from the present. That would be daydreaming. Tomorrow is a destination. If you know what you want, and want it badly enough, you'll use the means to pursue it now, or, to put it another way, future desires motivate you to fight in the present. No one guarantees that you will achieve your goal. No matter how many motivational phrases promise you that there's nothing you can't achieve if you try hard enough, experience shows that the slogan is just not true. And yet that's not an excuse for not trying. It is worth fighting for the future, because what experience also shows is that wandering on through the present without any goals makes for a very dull life indeed.

This search for the future starting in the present can occur in many areas of life: the pursuit of a personal calling, which will be discussed later; skills training, with the sacrifice involved, for the sake of future excellence; developing personal relationships, which cannot be reduced to the present alone, devoid of past memories or future projection.

Along with responsibility and motivation, the third element that the future offers is hope. Without hope, it's impossible to live. Hope is a fundamental force in human beings. It is so necessary that it pulls you through when the present becomes dark, arid or gloomy. *Carpe diem* still has a meaning when the present is sparkling and joyful, when life smiles at you, problems aren't dragging you down, humour accompanies you and relationships work. But what about when it doesn't? What about when the sky is overcast, and the storm breaks over your head? What if difficulties weigh down on you, if you're dancing with sadness or if love goes astray? Do difficulties rob you of your sleep, your patience and your hope? If the only thing that matters is the present moment, then that stormy present will be a ravening monster that demands immediate solutions. Everything will take a back seat except the need to feel happy again as soon as possible.

The fact is that it's often not possible, or it's not even desirable. Because there are situations and problems that are objective, that don't have any immediate solution and that require patience.

Hope is a look at the future that leads us to fight in the present, with the ability to endure the portion of desert and darkness that our present may entail. Hope is not naive escapism but a way of looking at the world clearly, looking at ourselves and others with confidence, and looking at time with patience.

Let's take an example. Ben Macintyre is an investigative journalist specialising in espionage stories of the Second World War. His biographies of some of the most fascinating characters of the war are fascinating. I found *Colditz: Prisoners of the Castle* particularly fruitful to read. Colditz was a prison-fortress, supposedly escape-proof, where the Germans incarcerated enemy army officers who had attempted to escape from other prisons. Between 1939 and 1945, Colditz was the scene of a cat-and-mouse game between the Nazis and the Allied prisoners-of-war. Meticulous escape plans, tunnels, unlikely disguises, surprising routes through roofs and basements were constantly being tried by the Allies and almost always foiled by their captors. Very few of these escapes were successful, but just one single victory was enough to inflame the prisoners, encouraging them to resist and to believe that it was possible to win even in their circumstances. The point of the story is the power of hope as a stimulus that enabled many of those prisoners to maintain their sanity, spirit of resistance and courage, despite the atrocious prison conditions and their inability to control the circumstances of their confinement.

This example also points up something else I think needs underlining in this dance with time. The maturity I'm talking about is not primarily a question of age. In your early twenties, you can act in an adult way and without losing the joyousness of youth. At the other extreme, there are people who are still superficial, rootless flirts long after they've left their youth behind. Some of the soldiers and officers imprisoned in Colditz were only twenty-two or twenty-three. It is true that we are talking about European society eighty years ago and in a war context. Life had already made them grow up. It was a time for being adults, without any golden cages or prolonged adolescence. But regardless of the context, I think it's true that learning this music of time is something very personal, even today. Some learn to dance with time from a very young age, and others don't seem able to get out of the immediate, trivial present, no matter how many years they have lived.

Composing a story

To finish off this chapter: ultimately, we don't live through a string of disconnected present moments. We are composing a story out of our decisions, our steps, the luggage we gather, the desires we make a place for, and the things and ideals that motivate us. In our story, the past, the present and the future dance. The three are intertwined, and there's a constant flow between them.

Memory helps us to retrieve what we have experienced in the past, which is part of what we are today. Hope teaches us to look ahead, even to a time when we are no longer here. And putting our heart into the present, here and now, helps us not to try and escape in either direction.

It seems to me that an adult is someone who has learned to live in a healthy relationship with all three times: someone who knows how to learn from yesterday without turning it into a labyrinth of nostalgia or reproaches; someone who is able to project towards the future, articulating desires, plans and possibilities in that look; someone who understands that you must identify and give a name to what you live through every day and not feel compelled to idealise the present. You can enjoy it when it is wonderful, and you understand that sometimes it won't be.

We human beings are creatures who are capable of telling stories and of knowing our own story. We're even capable of writing it down and trying to give it a direction (which doesn't mean we can determine it).

Perhaps this awareness of the passage of time is one of our greatest abilities. That's why it's so important to respect our own history – both our personal one and the collective one – without rewriting it to serve particular interests, contemporary ideologies or political correctness. That's why forgetting can be so dangerous, personally and socially. And that's why not thinking about the long term and the consequences of decisions made today can be so tragic for our future life.

The history of each person is not just an objective description of events. It is also a dance with time, woven from decisions, learning, purposes, encounters and farewells.

6

Let Yourself Be Surprised

Who can say, at forty, that their life has become what they dreamed of at twenty? We can plan and wish. We can take steps in a certain direction. We can make our preparations, but the truth is that the world will always be unpredictable and much bigger than our desires, goals and expectations. Your story will never cease to surprise you. There's a well-known saying, 'If you want to make God laugh, tell him your plans.' Mind you, it's not that God is going to spitefully ruin those plans, and that's why he laughs, but that God, in his wisdom, knows perfectly well that reality is going to surprise you.

There's so much you don't know about yourself, about others and about the society you live in, and there's so much that isn't up to you, that you have no way of controlling; life won't stop giving you surprises. Aiming to have everything clear, aiming to have planned things down to the last detail and already know everything at a certain moment, aiming to know what fate has in store for you – all that is a vain attempt to achieve a degree of certainty that is both impossible and unnecessary.

When someone looks back and speaks to their younger self, one piece of advice they usually give is that they should be open to surprises, because the future is unpredictable. This is how an Argentine seminarian, now a priest, spoke to his younger self.

> My name is Santi. I'm twenty-six, and I am training for the priesthood; I'm a seminarian in Buenos Aires. If I had the opportunity to speak to Santi ten years ago and give him some advice, I think this is what I would say.

Brother, you're fifteen, and you're not at your best right now, I know …

One word that describes you (I see it everywhere in you – in your eyes, in what you think, in what you feel, in your classes, in your sports, in your friends, in your time out, in your body) is 'confusion'. And today, I want to offer you a different word.

OK, but don't close yourself off against the word I'm going to tell you! Seriously, I'm telling you ten years later. You're going to think I'm delirious, that I don't know what I'm saying, that I don't understand your situation, but ten years later, I'm telling you – and I'm not delirious, I do know what I'm saying, I do understand your situation and I feel with you everything you're going through, but, even so, and precisely for that reason, today I want to tell you: 'You're going to be surprised.'

It's so good to be able to meet you! To be able to get close to you and give you a word of encouragement! To be able to appear in the middle of your life, which is a bit closed off, to calm things down. How much I'd like to help you relax! To prick the bubble of your nightmares, which could become hells.

If you saw my beard, you'd get an idea of how things change – even your face itself! If you saw my smile, you wouldn't believe it. If you saw my excited eyes piercing you with a serene, compassionate and much more confident look, you wouldn't recognise them. Of course, not everything is rosy today either; we didn't get from there to here by coming through a magic door. But how good it is to be able to meet you today and tell you, 'You're going to be surprised!' I assure you, I beg you: open yourself up to surprise! Because it's coming, and it's coming to give you a lot and to promise you much more, giving it to you little by little, over time.

In the confusion of your body, you'll get the surprise of feeling at home.

In the confusion of your feelings, the surprise of a harmony that can tame any beast.

In the confusion of your studies, the surprise of a vocation – which you never expected – that unfolds to offer you far more than you could ever have imagined, even if you'd invented your own profession.

In the confusion of your relationships, the surprise of a huge capacity to love, and to be immeasurably loved, chosen and forgiven … You're going to meet people you've never seen before! Many of them will form part of your deep joy, and you will transform many others.

In the confusion of your falls, the surprise of new opportunities, not only to get up, but to walk, run and dance.

In the confusion of your loneliness and the confusion of your emptiness, the surprise of a deeper presence that accompanies you closely through any desert; the surprise of a fullness that, although you can't always taste it, is always enough to keep you alive along the way.

You're doing well, little brother. If this time is a storm, know that the harvest is coming, a harvest that the storm watered and that the years made grow. Know that, despite this grey season, you can continue believing in the God of Life, in the God who heals broken hearts. A harvest is coming that will surprise you! A catch so abundant that you'll think your nets are about to burst! I promise you, you'll be surprised.[9]

He's not the only one who, looking back, recognises that life brings unexpected harvests. The ability to let oneself be surprised is not by any means reserved just for adults. It can happen at every stage of life. The surprise is like that, unpredictable, original, unexpected. It bursts in when and where you did not expect it.

9. S. Obiglio, 'How, in your confusions, you will be surprised', pastoralsj.org, https://pastoralsj.org /being/1876-confusiones-te-vas-a-sorprender.

Childhood is, almost by definition, the time of constant surprise, in which everything is new. As a child you wonder, you get scared, you discover, you investigate and you ask again and again about everything that is beyond. You sense that the world is infinite.

Then you grow up, and I'm not saying that when you're older you think you know everything. But it can happen that at some point, due to impatience, a too narrow focus or overload, you restrict your thoughts to what you know, what you've got and what you've heard of. You think that's quite enough for you.

From the point of view of being open to surprises, maturing doesn't mean being satisfied with the same old things, nor reducing life to the present alone. It doesn't mean saying, 'This far and no further', 'That's all there is to life', and 'I've nothing left to learn.'

Maturing is about assuming you're ignorant about almost everything – about others, about the world, about God and about yourself – and, precisely for that reason, understanding that reality is an area where you can continue growing, believing and learning.

Life's going to surprise you, whether you want it to or not. Names that you never imagined are waiting for you in the future. How could you possibly think, right now, about the people whose stories may cross paths with yours at some stage? About the experiences that will make you touch the sky or crash to the ground? About the problems that will confront you, and the ones that you'll solve? About how projects you're working on right now will come to fruition? And about how others you don't yet know about will emerge? About how you will react to new, as yet unknown events?

The wonderful thing is that, even when less of the road still lies ahead, there will still be blank pages where you don't know what will be written. Even death will come with a dose of surprise. And your way of approaching it may make you discover parts of yourself that you don't yet intuit.

Some people's lives seem frozen into immobility, as if they have stopped hoping, and that problem could menace you, if you're the dissatisfied, sad type who avoids thinking about the future so as not to get depressed. But it could equally be your problem, if you're an incorrigible optimist and think that you already live in the best of all possible worlds, because in that case you'll be setting the bar of possibilities too low.

Don't cling permanently to what you already know about. So much is going to change that it would be a shame to stop being open to novelty too soon.

Two attitudes are basic to living open to surprise.

One is the awareness of how much you don't know. There is nothing sadder than that sterile attitude of someone who seems to know everything. Whether you're talking about politics, religion, economics, psychology, football, the pope's new encyclical or the latest fashion series – you've already analysed everything, explained everything. What a pity! Because the reality is that you, all of us, are very ignorant about almost everything. It's no big deal. We're ignorant because we haven't had a chance to find out, because we weren't born with an instruction manual under our arm, because our capacity to learn is limited. But at the same time, we're creatures who learn, capable of continuing to grow and opening ourselves to what is new. However, some people obstinately insist on giving an opinion on everything without giving themselves the space or opportunity to learn, to listen and to embrace something new!

When you do know the ins and outs of a topic, and you see, for example, on social networks, habitual opinion-givers demonstrating their ignorance with an air of confidence, you can't help thinking how brazen stupidity is. How much noise it makes, and how little it helps when someone claims to know everything. There are few expressions more liberating than the simple admission, 'I don't know.'

Awareness of our own ignorance is of little use, except perhaps to help us be more humble, if it isn't linked to the very human sense of curiosity. That's the second essential attitude: a desire to learn, to open ourselves to something new, a willingness to never stop growing. That is a human capacity that lifts us above ourselves – our eagerness to know, a concern to go beyond the borders of what we're familiar with, an awareness that something new can emerge, and the freedom to not chain ourselves to certainties for fear of the elements.

Surprise isn't just about knowledge. It's much more about experiences. So often, doors will open for you that you didn't expect to go through, and answers will appear to questions that you don't even know you're asking yourself.

When you look back you're surprised to discover how much you've changed and how much the world you live in has changed. Sometimes for the better, and sometimes for the worse. Who could have told the sceptic that one day he would regain his faith or the dogmatist that one day her doubts would make her grow? Who would have told the lonely man that one day he would find the love he had dreamed of and that it would be much better than he imagined? Who would have told the student that one day she would be a storyteller? How could the aspiring criminal imagine that he would end up giving his life to others? Who was the first to imagine the internet, the networks, artificial intelligence? Who could have told us a few years ago that we would have to live through a pandemic, see the streets of the world empty while we wondered what would become of us? Who could have said how some projects into which we put our heart and soul and life would end? Not all surprises are good, but we absolutely need to know how to face the unexpected, in order to welcome what is a blessing and in order to cope with what hurts.

Let's change the verb tense. Let's look from the present to the future. What new names will figure in your life? Who will you have to share projects with, and friendship, intuitions, conversation, confidences, laughter and some tears? Where are those people now? Maybe you meet them every day on the street, without knowing that one day they'll be so important to you. What new places will you go to, that today you can't even imagine visiting? What new inventions will you live to see, in this world that is changing at dizzying speed? What songs will you learn by heart? What books, maybe being written right now as you read these words, will thrill you one day as you recognise yourself in the characters and make you understand some of the battles you've been fighting without realising it? Will the world improve, or get worse?

Of course, as was said earlier about the past, not all your future surprises will be pleasant ones. You'll be hurt and shocked. Events will take place that you'd prefer not to have to handle. You'll shudder at tragedies that haven't yet happened. Your own weakness and vulnerability will be proved in unsuspected ways.

That's what life is all about, and when your time comes to suffer you'll know that it isn't the end of the story, because life is a series of changes. The unexpected does happen, and recognising the existence of variability, novelty and unimagined new things is a real gift.

Sometimes when we get stuck in a rut, accept defeat or get the feeling that there's nothing new under the sun, we need to remind ourselves that anything can happen, right up to the very end.

As believers, even in the way we live out our faith, we have to be open to newness. God is the God of surprises.[10] A God who, when you think you know him, catches you unawares all over again. A God who, when you think you're following him, switches you onto a new track. A God who, when you think you can talk about him, leaves you speechless. The images that perhaps helped you explain him once become insufficient, and others then help you to understand him better, respond to him better and find more meaning in the world you live in. There is nothing sadder than turning faith into a museum visit where everything is already set out in a detailed catalogue of its contents. And there's nothing more sterile than the rigidity which, in the name of a misunderstood tradition, blocks off every path to change.

As believers we have the responsibility, I'd even say the obligation, to dialogue with this changing world. Our dialogue is not merely speaking of immutable truths in the right language for new contexts. It is also an ability to let those new contexts light up our way of understanding the revelation on which our beliefs are based. And that is not relativism, nor does it involve letting ourselves be swept away by the politically correct mindset of each succeeding age. It means refusing to claim that we already know all that there is to be known about the world, human beings and God.

10. Gerard Hughes, *God of Surprises* (London: Darton Longman & Todd, 2008).

7

No Disagreement Allowed

A world made to measure

Wouldn't it be nice to live in a world that was made to measure, especially for you? Think about this before you answer. Maybe your immediate answer would be, 'Yes, of course!' Who wouldn't like the world to match up to what we ourselves wanted? Imagine: clothes that fit you like a glove. Being able to eat whatever you most like at whatever time you choose. Every kind of product designed to your specifications and measurements. Leaders, from the local mayor right up to the pope in Rome if you're a Catholic, who see the world the same way as you do, in everything you're concerned about, and who keep to the line you expect of them. People who think the same way as you do, so every discussion ends in perfect agreement. Education that doesn't demand too much of you. Conditions that match your desires in every sphere of life: work, thought, leisure, consumption, everything. The kind of music you enjoy, always correctly selected for you by algorithms that know your tastes. Films and series that entertain you, without your having to wade through a thousand different suggestions. Personalised recommendations on all your networks, so you don't have to put up with content that doesn't interest you. And, of course, no toxic personalities around you, or even anyone you don't get on with.

However, what may well sound like a very pleasant world, harmonious, comfortable and secure, turns out to be a nightmare as soon as you scratch below the surface. That placid comfort involves a stifling homogeneity and gives you a growing inability to cope with conflict, difference or, taken to extremes, even the slightest setback. And it also makes it impossible for you to grow or change, since there are no fixed limits or external points of reference to shake you out of your familiar circuits.

Even if we thought that a world made to our measure would be desirable, and if we weren't too bothered about growing and changing – it isn't possible. For the simple reason that reality is complex, people are different, and our surroundings impose limitations that we have to take into account. I am not the measure of reality. My desires and tastes are not the laws that rule the universe.

Yet how tempting it is to think of a world without any difficulties or setbacks! But dreaming of a world like that means denying the need for conflict, disagreement and upsets in life. Such dreamers seem to be saying, 'I have the right to have not a single second of discomfort. I have the right to have nothing that makes me uncomfortable. I have the right not to waste a moment listening to opinions that make me feel uneasy.'

Is there a time for everything, as the earlier quotation from Ecclesiastes said? It seems not. There's no time for listening to what I don't like, facing up to what I don't agree with, or dialoguing with worldviews that are different from my own. There's no room for alternative choreographies in this world that is made to my measure.

The attempt to create a world with apparently no room for any disappointment or frustration was very well presented over twenty-five years ago in the film *Pleasantville*, which offered an interesting metaphor for the whole question. It showed two contrasting worlds: that of David and Jennifer, twins living in an ordinary American town, and that of the idyllic – or unbearable, depending on how you look at it – world of Pleasantville. This world is in black and white, and is like a television serial, where everything is controlled and predictable, children love their parents, the husbands go out to work and their wives look after the house. Young people are all well behaved. Life is comfortable. Love is all under control. Books are all blank – after all, new ideas are not needed. When you leave the town on one side, the road brings you round and back in at the other – nobody has ever left Pleasantville. The future will be exactly as foreseen.

By a strange chance, David and Jennifer are transported into Pleasantville and become inhabitants of this TV world. The twins' arrival shows up two ways of understanding life. David feels at home in this new world. He loves its orderliness and could perfectly well become a model citizen of the black-and-white town, where everything is totally predictable. Jennifer, unlike him, is not prepared to let herself be tamed by this nightmare universe. She thinks differently, behaves freely and wants something different.

Through their contact with Jennifer some of Pleasantville's inhabitants begin to realise that there are many feelings that they never express, many desires that they have been leaving unrecognised, and that the world may be much wider than what there is in their narrow minds. As they start letting the truth emerge, colours begin to appear in them and their surroundings. The idyllic, black-and-white town turns into a place of sharp contrasts. And these in their turn bring conflict between the black-and-white citizens and the in-colour citizens, because now not everyone thinks the same or has the same goals. Sometimes one person's freedom clashes with another person's selfishness. Some want the freedom of unpredictability, and others want the security of what is familiar. And this conflict cannot be avoided.

The film ends with a shout for a world in colour, complex life, unpredictability, the capacity to learn and conflict with a reality that often exceeds our abilities and skills at any given moment. That's what gives us the capacity to grow.[11]

I don't mind saying that today, by other means and using other discourses, we run the risk of returning to Pleasantville. Or at least, that there are plenty of people who would like to. A black-and-white world where everyone shares the same convictions, securities and ways of thinking. A world where nobody ever has to face difficulties or be met with a flat 'no', even though, in order to achieve this, every form of dissidence has to be suppressed.

---

11. *Pleasantville* courtroom scene clip, https://www.youtube.com/watch?v=zd0Ce0-_pJg.

Don't contradict, it upsets me

Adult life has to be able to deal with complexity, and the resulting plurality, but in fact we live in times of pervasive immaturity in which anything to do with diversity and conflict is very badly handled.

Is it understandable that there are times in the journey to maturity when one tends towards dualism, seeing everything as either black or white, with no greyscale? Yes. We may have been through that stage ourselves, but a time comes when it has to be left behind, as we comprehend that the world is more nuanced and that people are different from each other, that I, my perceptions and my opinions, are not the measure of all things. And that to a certain extent, out of a combination of honesty, survival instinct, clear-headedness and even kindness, I have to learn to adapt to the world I live in without trying to make everything in it fit in with my tastes or convenience.

If we look at the field of education, we easily find examples of how some approaches today are preventing children from developing enough resilience to handle setbacks. Some teaching methods are geared towards protecting children from any kind of difficulty, preventing them from experiencing failure or facing up to the demands of a tough task, and even want to spare them the effort of learning anything by heart and so developing the capacities of their memory. The excuse that is given for this is that today we have everything available anyway, so why should children waste their energy on accumulating concepts or information that they can easily access at any given moment?

When new education schemes aim to abolish the possibility of failure, and when there are enormous disputes around making a schoolchild or student repeat a year, in the hopes of finding a better way to motivate them, are young people really being prepared for adult life? We need to be trained to face a world where we'll have to dance with success and failure. Where sometimes we will put persistence, effort and enthusiasm into goals that we won't achieve (although other times we will). Where sometimes we'll be overwhelmed by circumstances. And where we'll often have to listen to things we don't like to hear.

Another source of conflict that is increasingly less recognised is the inability to manage differences of opinion. Many people's basic attitude is that anyone who doesn't hold the same positions as me about a controversial issue is or soon will be my enemy. In many areas, people have simply lost the ability to talk about differences of opinion without making it personal, and have become hypersensitive, taking any 'no' as an act of aggression.

In *The Coddling of the American Mind*, Jonathan Haidt and Greg Lukianoff reflect on the growing inability to tolerate disagreement in contemporary society.[12] They focus on something that has been happening for years in North American universities and that has led to what is known as the 'cancel culture'. It says that I have the right to prevent people I don't agree with from expressing themselves. They have no right to upset me with their opinions. It's not just that I have the right not to listen to them; I have the right to prevent them from speaking at all, anywhere where I may chance to be. As blunt as that.

These authors reflect on three attitudes that have been causing an absurd degree of emotion in many areas of today's society.

First, there is the fear that a statement will hurt me. I have the right to protect myself against anything that makes me feel bad, whether it is non-inclusive language, prejudices or all approaches that are different from mine. If something offends me, the problem belongs to whoever says it (regardless of whether I have very thin skin), and therefore any topic that I may consider hurtful has no right to exist. I have the right to silence the other person, because I do not want to hear what they want to say.

Secondly, as discussed earlier, there has been a shift from reason to emotion as a criterion of truth. Today, in too many areas, emotional reasoning reduces truth to feelings: if I feel it, it's true, or anyway it's my truth, regardless of the data. If I feel bad about what you say, my feeling is the truth. Your words, therefore, have to be outlawed.

---

12. Jonathan Haidt and Greg Lukianoff, *The Coddling of the American Mind: How Good Intentions and Bad Ideas Are Setting Up a Generation for Failure* (London and New York: Penguin, 2019).

Thirdly, our contemporary dualism turns the conflict into a battle between the good guys and the bad guys, heightened by everyone's conviction that they themselves are the 'good guys', demonising their opponents along the way.

This triple whammy, in the United States, has taken over the intellectual world of the universities above all (and surprisingly) and has rendered people incapable of true argument and debate. This is especially worrying, because in the academic sphere reflection ought to be much more nuanced and thoughtful, and arguing, or the exchange of opposite ideas, is not merely something that should be possible but is necessary. The imposition of a politically correct way of thinking that stifles true freedom of thought has been extremely rapid. Many people have been banned, sanctioned or erased from the agenda of many institutions for defending ideas that could displease a potential audience.

And of course the phenomenon described by Haidt and Lukianoff is not restricted to American universities. It is spreading throughout the world, starting with Europe. Just ask the author J. K. Rowling, who has been dropped from countless media outlets, including advertising for the *Harry Potter* saga, for her opinions on the 'trans issue'. It is also reaching Spain, unfortunately, not only in classrooms, but also around family tables, on social networks, in many media outlets and in parliament. As Fernando Bonete said in an interesting analysis of cancel culture, 'Any reaction to disagreement that doesn't involve dialogue leads to censorship.'[13] But censorship, and self-censorship, is more and more in evidence as a means to avoid problems and persecution by the media.

It is clear that freedom of expression cannot be an excuse for any statement whatever. Some statements should definitely not be acceptable. A good criterion for the limits of how far one can go is the law. But only as long as the law doesn't also end up becoming a new cultural inquisition, so that democracy deteriorates into ideological dictatorship – something that can't be ruled out either, these days.

The problem is that political correctness right now is drawing the line a long way in advance of what is lawful. Today, people are offended by

---

13. F. Bonete Vizcaíno, *La cultura de la cancelación* (Madrid: Ciudadela, 2023), p. 79.

comedians' politically incorrect jokes, and immediately media attacks are unleashed against the offending comedians until they apologise and promise to make amends and not to repeat the offence, for fear of being cancelled.

Perhaps the slap Will Smith gave Chris Rock at the 2022 Oscars, when Rock made an ill-considered joke about Smith's wife's alopecia, shows this rapid escalation and inability to tackle differences or conflicts in any mature way. It was still way over the top, and you can't build a whole thesis on one incident like that, but I think it helps to see, graphically, how inter-personal tension is gaining ground. Perhaps we haven't yet reached the point where it's seen as normal to resolve disagreements by physical blows, and in this case the person who ended up being cancelled for a long season was Will Smith. But it's still true that today, society seems like a powder-keg, ready to explode at the slightest spark.

An influencer having a bad day, an out-of-place comment or an ill-judged tweet, and yesterday's hero is today's public enemy. We can laugh at the pulpits and the morality control of yesteryear. Today there are new inquisitions of political correctness and new anathemas to indoctrinate followers and silence dissidents. Contemporary autos-da-fé don't include bonfires, but they're getting there fast.

Today people who disagree with a politician organise noisy protests to prevent them from being heard. Famous writers are censored for having their own opinions, if they differ from those of the implacable majority, and are given no opportunity to explain them or defend their right to hold them. The possibility of dissent or debate is denied. Presentations by uncomfortable speakers are cancelled to avoid conflict.

The television series *Black Mirror* has explored many different scenarios, playing with possible future directions technology could take. One of the most disturbing ideas it has developed has to do precisely with a warped form of cancellation. In 'White Christmas', a special Christmas episode released in 2014, it plays with the possibility of blocking people, not on social networks but in real life. Could it be possible, in a world where we are increasingly interconnected with our own devices, to make the other invisible, inaudible and unreachable? Would it be possible, as in that episode, for a woman to block her ex-husband in such a way that he cannot see or hear his family, or be seen or heard by them? Or, worse still, could a criminal be punished by being literally blocked out from everyone?

The fury grows

As the capacity for disagreement and rational debate is lost in the areas where it should be most accepted (though, as pointed out above, this goes far beyond universities), polarisation increases. This happens because, no matter what efforts are made to bring the world in line with homogeneous beliefs and single perspectives, people are different. And since we can't now accept differences, we become entrenched in our own views. Much of contemporary populism has to do with this.

One of the most fiercely fought battles in contemporary society is the battle for 'discourse' or 'story'. This is understood as the pressure by different social agents to establish interpretations of reality that favour their interests, ideologies or different visions of the world. This is very evident in the field of politics, where convincing the voter that your views are the right ones can tip the balance between success and power on the one hand or irrelevance and oblivion on the other. But it also shows up in other areas, in these days when truth is not much valued. We can find these dynamics in the Church (will the defenders of synodality win or those who ridicule it?), in culture (some of the positions in the so-called 'cultural war' – not all – come from here) and in all public analysis of conflicts large and small.

Whether we're talking about feminism, gender issues, pro-life, abuse, the Europa League or fear of foreigners, everything has become a matter of opinion. With the added difficulty that the overarching narratives that once provided a common ground, such as the religious worldview or famous ideologies, have become so blurred or fragmented as to lose all consistency.

Particular discourses seem to weigh more in public opinion than reality. Politics today is conducted with slogans more than with laws. Political advisors gain their positions because they are opinion-makers not because they are experts in public policy.

The alarming thing is that disagreement leads instantly to rupture. There is no longer any room for discordant speeches and voices within the same movement: each difference of opinion leads to splits and an ever-greater fragmentation of society.

What I've been describing so far is a recognised social phenomenon, the dynamics of which affect the media, social networks, institutions and public discourse. The bad thing is that it also ends up affecting people in more everyday areas. Inability to manage difference, to accept conflict, to live with different discourses or even discuss them is leading to a world of people who are incapable of understanding complexity or accepting any kind of contradiction.

Social networks are a good example of the sort of dynamics that this generates. You find people who are incapable of accepting that others think differently and who resort to violent polemics in order to silence them. Differing views lead immediately to attacks on the other person, refusing them the right to speak. An inability to perceive nuances, producing over-simplifications and incomprehension. Loves and hates. Sectarianism. Searching for like-minded groups to bolster your position. An inability to see or understand the reasons and arguments of those who think differently from you.

All of this is happening. I understand that there is no reason to put up with many things. That sometimes you have to draw a line to protect yourself from thugs or polemicists who are only looking for trouble.

I can protect myself from some speeches that hurt me. I can distance myself. I can even silence or block, on my networks, people who insult, provoke or constantly upset. What I cannot do is claim they have no right to exist. And that is what is happening, explicitly or covertly, by labelling those who think differently, trying to expel or silence them, or denying their right to think differently.

A British journalist and writer, Douglas Murray, a few years ago aptly coined the term 'the madness of crowds'[14] to describe this state of mind,

---

14. Douglas Murray, *The Madness of Crowds: Gender, Race and Identity* (London: Bloomsbury, 2019). In the book, the author applies his analysis especially to confrontations in the areas of identity politics and gender issues, but there is no doubt that what he describes can be applied to many other areas of public life.

which is gaining more and more followers. I would even talk about 'the fury of the mob'. People are irascible, susceptible, hair-trigger sensitive. Everything is dramatised.

As a Catholic, I am going to allow myself a digression. I believe that this is also happening in the Church. It is sad, because as Catholic faithful we should be able to accommodate differences, nuances and the complexity of all human situations. And in fact, historically, we have done so. What are the different spiritualities and charisms that have had such a long history in the Church other than different paths and ways of seeing reality? Of course, very different perceptions, sensibilities, views and discourses have always coexisted – and sometimes clashed. This hasn't been a problem but has been part of the true value of a two-thousand-year-old institution, where very different approaches have all had their place. However, today there are many defenders of a misunderstood orthodoxy (and I don't mean just orthodoxy as in magisterium but also an 'orthodox progressivism', if we go along with those inadequate labels), apologists for a rigid homogeneity, dogmatists of all content and persecutors of dissidents. They are also at home on social networks.

Rants, merciless criticism, disrespect, anathemas and condemnations, as if we were once again involved in the religious wars that bled Europe dry a few centuries ago. They use the same tactics as any other angry group. Like packs of hounds they attack anyone who goes off-script. It would be sad, if it weren't also a little scary, to see where this state of affairs leads.

Few things seem more immature to me than this all-out rigidity. I don't know if there has ever been more talk of 'tolerance' from positions of such entrenched intolerance – so many insults used as labels for others. Labels are being used so crudely that they are either normalised or lose all meaning. Just think how quickly people call large parts of the population 'fascist'. How easily someone with different views on a nation, a language or conflict resolution is called a 'traitor'. Someone who argues that certain moral issues need re-thinking is called 'degenerate', and someone who asks for more careful thought on those issues instead of rushing to change the law is labelled 'retrograde' or 'traditionalist'.

In some cases, these labels may hold some truth, but in most cases, they are the result of the anger that has taken root within us.

All this happens every day, in all the media and every part of the spectrum of ideologies. It's not only embarrassing and sad, but it also leaves people fragile, very easily manipulated and very dependent on official opinions.

Relax!

What can be done about the implacably black-and-white attitudes that result from a combination of dualism, inability to see the other side's viewpoints and over-sensitivity? First, we ourselves need to recover our calm. This doesn't mean we should fall into relativism, and I'm not saying that every belief is equally good, or that life doesn't involve some battles that are legitimate and necessary. I mean that we need to clearly recognise that normally all the arguments are not on one side. What's more, society can't be built or maintained on the basis of constant quarrels and nor can anyone's personal life.

Please understand that here I'm not advocating the lazy calm of people who seem to have water in their veins instead of blood. We all know people who sometimes need to be shaken up, until they display a little more passion, fire, intensity or even anger. Of course there are times in life when you have to be intense and committed, when difference does involve conflict, and when, to defend what is important to you, you will have to dialogue, argue and even fight. But it's not right that any difference whatsoever now leads to confrontation, or that the only way to avoid it is to cancel the other person.

What we need to do is take the time and calmness to manage difference, to assume that there are times when we will have to go through stages of conflict. Because, quite often, covering up differences of opinion or being afraid to argue and disagree ends up causing a false peace that only masks the problems and even makes them more acute.

There are certain approaches that can help people to distance themselves a little from the pervasive culture of anger.

The first is respect. It turns out that, yes, there are people who have different ideas than ours: other values, other ways of understanding life, relationships, education, faith … And we have to live together in pluralistic societies. The real limits are the law and human rights, but we have to be careful not to make the law into a tool at the service of our personal tastes. There is a temptation these days to legislate on many issues that will impact on other people's lives just because the lawmakers so choose. Respect means giving others the right to have their opinions and understanding that they can make choices in accordance with those opinions.

The second is flexibility. You have to be a bit flexible when dealing with different people, in different situations and with all sorts of different opinions. What's more, nowadays you have to make the effort to listen to them, because otherwise those accursed algorithms will feed you more and more content that matches your own tastes and reinforces your own opinions. Above all, you have to be flexible so as not to turn everyday issues into problems or dramas. At the beginning of the Covid-19 lockdown, I was very struck by how, for a few surprising weeks, the shared emergency put things into perspective, smoothed out rough edges and allowed us to recognise in each other the same basic, very human determination to cope. Back then, many of the usual conflicts seemed totally insignificant, and we felt much closer and more akin to each other. Unfortunately the mirage of unity didn't last long. As soon as there was room for action, we went back to our guns.

Being flexible doesn't mean pretending that 'it all comes to the same thing' or that every statement has equal value. Flexibility is about recognising that there are conflicting approaches in any society and then finding ways to deal with them that don't involve confrontation or cancelling.

Flexibility is needed, for example, to reach agreement in politics. That's something that is increasingly complicated in this polarised world. Flexibility is also needed to be able to make progress in dialogues in the context of the Church, so that people don't immediately react against any attempt at clarification as if it was a kind of relativism.

Another very healthy attitude is a sense of humour. We ought to laugh a lot at ourselves and how pompous we can become. We ought to laugh at our imaginary dramas and even smile at some of the real ones, which are not really so bad. A sense of humour is a form of resistance, criticism and perspective. Obviously humour can be as destructive as anger if used aggressively. And if it's misplaced or ill-judged (which unfortunately does happen), even humour can degenerate into anger. If we can't learn to laugh a little, we'll end up hitting anyone whose joke makes us feel bad – just ask Will Smith.

We need to learn to joke gently, even elegantly, knowing which red lines we don't want to cross. But with that caveat, I hope that we can learn to laugh a lot in this life and not with the bitter laughter of indifference or sarcasm. Laugh with other people. Laugh at how absurd this world sometimes is. Laugh at nonsense that, if we take it seriously, drives us crazy. And, above all, laugh at ourselves, at how absurd we can become, how fragile our pose of invulnerability is! What inflated egos we sometimes have! What a fight we put up because we refuse to admit that we are sad, or hurt or in need!

Humour is not resignation; it's resistance. It doesn't mean keeping quiet in the face of abuse or wrong-doing but rather responding with imagination, wit, subtlety and, if possible, intelligence.

The good thing about humour is that, where it's possible, it's a way of maintaining bridges, connections, between people.

True coexistence is not lots of like-minded people living together in a homogeneous world but people capable of accepting differences and still respecting each other. Convince yourself, you're going to have to live and work with many difficult people. Don't make it impossible from the outset.

Being an adult, at least in the sense that I'm putting forward in this little book, means learning to live with differences of opinion, taking tolerance seriously and not reducing it to a sad parody that contradicts in practice what it claims to be, accepting contradiction from someone without turning them into an enemy and learning to dialogue instead of wanting to make the dialogue into nothing but a many-voiced monologue.

8

At the Centre of My Life

Who are *you* dancing with? We all need to name the dance partners, or groups, who appear in our lives over time. Does dancing mean spinning round on oneself like a spinning-top? Dancing like that would be much too boring. Nor is dancing just staying static in one place while everything else moves and spins around. And although sometimes we may need to dance alone, other times we need more. Dancing without anyone else isn't enough for us. It gives us a feeling of incompleteness. When we dance, in some way we are carrying many other names, faces and stories with us. Our despair or our joy, our hope or our storm, all of this is with reference to other people.

No, life doesn't consist of isolating ourselves from the world, nor is it about becoming the centre of the universe. It's far more beautiful to move, to dance around other figures, interacting with one another. Dancing can be encounter, openness to knowledge, a dance-step shared with many others together.

Life is not a performance in which you are always the principal dancer, surrounded by spectators who applaud, cheer and wait for every step you take to praise you for doing it so well.

Today we live in a world that tries to turn us all into divas and prima donnas, and it's very easy to fall into that trap if we let ourselves. I sometimes think that growing up also means progressively broadening our vision to include others. I once read an article that gave a curious description of the baby as a human being who at first is naturally, and absolutely, turned in on itself, while discovering the world around it.

At the beginning, say the experts, the baby is infinite. A newborn does not end anywhere. She is not, they say, aware of any boundaries, and she makes no distinction between herself and the air, or her mother's breast, or gravity, or the cold. She wouldn't pick things up with her hands, even if she could, because she herself is those things, and she doesn't know where she ends and the rest begins, because for her 'the rest' doesn't exist. She is everything. And the sheets move, and the warmth of her mother's skin moves away, in just the same way as her tummy hurts or she defecates: because that's how her infinite body works, without her ever being able to control it. Then, little by little, she begins to learn that she is not her mother's breast, and that she needs to call for it, and that there are other faces in the air that bend over her cradle and they are not her. She begins to become aware of her limits and her hands, and of the difference between holding her feet and the toys that appear and disappear around her.

She learns to move, to crawl, to walk, within what was once her unlimited organism, and to move through it. She learns to look, as an act distinct from introspection or from her own consciousness. She is learning many things, poor little mite. Perhaps the most terrible day of her life is the day she learns to say 'Mummy'. What an immense loss! What an complete renunciation! Accepting that Mummy is not me, and finally recognising it, calling her, admitting her existence outside of myself ...

From that moment on, a long series of renunciations begins. We begin to call things by their name, separating them irreversibly from ourselves.[15]

I don't know if this description is correct in terms of developmental psychology, but it's certainly suggestive.

15. A. Burgueño, '*Dónde está todo*', *Sal Terrae*, 97 (2009), 23–33, p. 28.

We can see time as an ally on the path that is our life, enabling us to abandon solitude and go out to meet others. To come to understand that the world is not a mirror where we can look at reflections of ourselves in other people, but that it is much more enriching to look outside, to discover those others we interact with, whose paths we cross, whom we brush up against and walk with. To find out who they are, learn to look intently into their lives and try to work out a different map of the world, in which those others have stories, names, worries, wounds, emergencies, desires and tastes that are so different from our own. To feel at peace and comfortable being part of that world in which we are not the centre.

We live in a time when learning to cultivate that gaze at the other is increasingly difficult.

The messages that put *me* at the centre of the world range from the crude to the subtle, but there is enormous pressure for each of us to constantly and tirelessly conjugate the self. I am worth it. I want it. I need it. I deserve it. I think about it. I expect it. I decide. I … A huge, hungry, insatiably demanding self. By contrast, learning to use 'him', 'her', 'them', to think in the third person and to be open to the plural, is infinitely more fruitful, but it is a difficult achievement in this age of vanity and ego.

Faulty ways of looking

What do you notice when you go out on the street, or when you enter a room full of people? What kind of images do you look at on social media? How do you watch a film? What catches your attention when you meet someone?

The world enters our lives through our eyes. We learn to see, and our eyes, the ways we look, hold intention, specific searches, and we focus on some things, some aspects, and not others. We train our gaze, of course. We spend a good part of our lives learning how to look. Isn't that what education is about, from the very early lessons at home until we specialise in some area that gives us keys to interpret the world?

Formal education is not the only or the main way of learning how to look. From a very young age we open ourselves to the world. And, today, I would say it's difficult to really reach the other. I would like to describe some insufficient ways of looking, faulty gazes, that are widespread today.

The self-centred way of looking

The self-centred gaze is the one proposed by advertising. It comes naturally, in any case. In advertising, the truly important thing is not the product. If it were, advertisers would strive to offer the most objective, accurate and complete information possible about what they're advertising. However nothing could be further from the truth. Advertisers seek to capture you, attract your attention, convince you that a certain product, service or experience is exactly what you want. You are the most important thing: your desire, your needs, your appetite or your happiness. Some slogans, such as Ikea's strapline in Spain, 'Welcome to the independent republic of your home', L'Oréal's 'Because You're Worth It', or the striking name of a Chanel perfume, 'Égoïste', reflect this approach. Advertising appeals to you, makes you the centre of the world. Your tastes rule. You make the rules. The world is made to measure for you. Products are, in reality, excuses, means to feed that enormous self that wants to feel in control.

The distancing way of looking

Another gaze is connected with the news. We have never been better informed than we are today, or, more precisely, we have never had so much information at our fingertips. The world enters our lives from the moment we turn on our mobile phones. We know, instantly, what's happening anywhere on our planet. And that can't be called a self-centred view. We see tornadoes, earthquakes, wars or tsunamis. We see protests in many corners of the world. We see old people dying alone. We watch upheavals in other people's families: weddings, divorces, children, infidelity, reconciliations. We watch idols with feet of clay and how they fall. We attend parliamentary battles and state summits. We witness epic rescues in the Mediterranean. We also, unfortunately, see what happens when those rescues don't get there in time and corpses pile up on the seashore. We see the hells, and we also see the paradises of our world. We know how much the stars of the moment earn. We listen to their thank-you speeches when they receive awards. And now that everything is recorded, we can replay those moments at will.

However, this way of looking is also defective. Because unless we find a way to remedy it, the world seen via a screen ends up being a distant world.

If the way of looking that advertisements teach us can be described as a self-centred way of looking, this gaze of twenty-four-hour world-wide news is a distancing one. Nothing affects us, because we feel it's somehow alien. The most that some tragic events do is generate a few days' headlines and cause collective shock, but the thresholds of indifference are getting increasingly higher. We get used to seeing everything through a screen, and this makes us into distant spectators.

Habit, distance and lack of depth are a very complicated combination that prevents us from getting to the heart of stories today.

The virtual way of looking

The third way of looking, which is found everywhere today, is the virtual gaze. It is a way of looking at people we know and people we don't, especially through social networks. So many people spend hours and hours these days looking at other people's photos, watching others exercise perfect bodies, cook delicious dishes, show surprising skills, fall down, kiss, propose, campaign for popular causes, dance, travel, tan on the beach, cry, describe their illnesses, share their grief, play with their pets, take on absurd challenges, try on clothes, joke, flirt, cut their hair, eat and, above all, dance.

Perhaps right now Instagram and TikTok are the greatest exponents, although not the only ones, of our strange ability to enter the lives of strangers. But this virtual gaze is necessarily incomplete. People only show what they want, or at least they aim to.

It's a world of clips, edits and filters, a world where all we see is the idealised version that people choose to project. There's not much spontaneity there. There's no real encounter either. It's just a fiction, a game of tricks and mirrors, a world that encourages comparison.

Reality and fantasy, truth and filter, spontaneity and preparation, authenticity and fiction, are all somehow mixed. And when you enter that game, two attitudes are possible. If you believe what you're seeing, you're choosing not to see reality and you're involving yourself in a world of deception. That's not good. And if, knowing that it's unreal, you insist on seeing the world through the filter of networks, then you're deliberately choosing escapism, but that ends up influencing how you perceive the world and how you perceive yourself as well.

We can't live outside of these gazes. In our world, advertising, the news, or other people's lives exposed on social networks are everywhere, and I would say inescapable. What we need to do is not stop there. We need to learn to go beyond all of that, because if we don't manage to burst the bubble, if we don't manage to look at the other truthfully, then life becomes a race to the death between enormous egos competing with each other.

So in order to make the transition to adult life, we need learn how to educate our way of seeing so that it is a broad gaze, capable of discovering the other person.

Educating our eyes

Perhaps one of the best-known characters in Holy Scripture, familiar to believers and non-believers alike, is the Good Samaritan in Luke's parable: the compassionate traveller who cares for a wounded man when supposedly more pious people have passed by (Lk 10:25–37).

What is interesting is that, in telling this story, Jesus is responding to the question asked by a teacher of the law: 'Who is my neighbour?'

Who is my neighbour? Who is the other, whose life touches mine? In today's world, where, as described in the previous section, our gaze is constantly turned towards ourselves, we badly need to learn to look outside and discover others.

This requires a series of lessons that have to do with our history, with the experiences we accumulate and how we learn to process them, and also, necessarily, with our own character and sensitivity, and, of course, with the education we've received.

It isn't easy today, when we are so subject to the insufficient ways of seeing set out in the previous section, to get outside of ourselves and understand that there is independent life out there.

What would be the main lessons we need in this discovery of the other?

Learning that the other is other

OK, saying that 'the other is other' is repetition, and it sounds like saying that the sun is the sun or the rain is rain. Does the repeated word mean anything? Yes, in this case it does. It's a warning not to make the other person into a mirror for just looking at ourselves in.

It's sometimes hard to take in the fact that the other person is more than their connection or relationship with me. That person is not just my friend, my girlfriend, my father, my line manager, my doctor, my employee, my parish priest, a member of my community or my neighbour. They're a person in their own right, with their own life, their problems, their relationships, their way of thinking, their life story and their background.

There is so much we don't know about other people. We need to realise that fact fully, so that we don't demand the same opinions or reactions from everyone, or assume similarities between us where there are none in reality.

Quite often we take conflicts as something personal, when they're not intended as such. Not everything in the other person's life revolves around me. Their bad reaction may have nothing to do with me, but may be the result of something that is worrying them at that precise moment. What I see as coldness may simply show that they're more serious by nature than I am. When they're silent, it may be because they want to distance themselves from me, but it may equally be because they have a stomach ache, or they're worried about their sick pet, or they've had an argument at work that is upsetting them.

It can sometimes happen that we live alongside someone or spend a lot of time with people, but they remain complete strangers to us. Not because we isolate ourselves from one another, but because of our lack of interest, or because we don't take the time to look deeply at them and their lives. It's not about meddling, snooping or wanting to gossip about other people's lives. It's something much more human. It's that primordial interest that brings to our lips, quite naturally, the question, 'And who are you?'

There's so much we don't know about others, and it's essential for us to realise it. Each person is a world. And no matter how well we get to know someone, we'll always only get halfway between the surface and that ultimate, intimate, personal depth, where only the self enters and through faith, if we let him, God.

Learning to see the other with their limitations

We can educate our gaze to see the other person's limitations without being condescending and without making undue demands on them. We live in a society of retouched images portraying unreal perfection, a society of shop windows that must show nothing but what is perfect.

What pressure we have put ourselves under with this need for endlessly giving opinions and evaluating others! Social networks are a good example of our society, where everyone seems to be somehow a judge in the reality show that is life and to spend their life rating others.

What freedom we find in realising, as time goes by, that we all have flaws. That the other has feet of clay, just as we do ourselves. To know that they get angry too, sometimes for no reason. That they sometimes make wrong decisions. That they react like a child when you would expect a little more maturity. That sometimes they're not as free as they want to appear, and just like you, have their own dependencies, their obsessions and their phobias.

Learning to accept defects – our own and other people's – is liberating. Embracing our own fragility, the contrast between our great words and our poor deeds. All of this frees us from the demand to measure up to impossible standards.

It doesn't mean that nothing really matters, or that we don't want to improve, but it does mean accepting that some changes will take time and effort, and that there are no guarantees, and that there are other limitations that are here to stay, because they're part of who we are as people.

Nobody's perfect, just as nobody is a total fraud. Every human being has their light and shadow aspects, their talents and their failings, their abilities and their limitations.

Perhaps that's one of the greatest transformations in culture in recent decades: the ever-increasing visibility of the contradictions in our heroes' characters. In literature, in films and in serials, the characters are mixed. Today we don't expect heroes like George Bailey, that man of integrity who, in *It's a Wonderful Life*, transformed a whole town by his honesty, his commitment to his neighbours and his innate goodness. Nor are the bad guys of today absolute villains. They have their hearts, their wounds and even their moments of hesitation or flashes of goodness. Today's hero is more ambiguous, like Walter White, the bored chemistry teacher who, wanting to secure his family's financial future, goes in for manufacturing methamphetamine and discovers that it's not so bad breaking bad.

However, the paradox is that, while we accept ambiguity in fictional characters, public discourse is increasingly dualistic. There are good guys and bad guys. People can't perceive any values in 'the enemy' or any faults or mistakes in 'the ally'.

As I've just said, accepting people's limitations doesn't mean that there's no such thing as good and bad, or that the fact that we are all human is sufficient justification for anything at all. We can't give in to the seduction of evil. I believe that a moral view of life is increasingly necessary. What I do say, though, is that we must learn to look at others, recognising their fragility, their weakness, their feet of clay. This is how to avoid entering a world of impossible expectations, excessive demands and summary judgements.

Learning to handle conflict

Just because we see that everyone has limitations, doesn't mean it's easy to accept them. That's precisely why we call them limitations, because in some way they seem to limit expectations, desires or aspirations towards achievement. And when it comes to little obsessions, quirks of character, communication difficulties, character defects and incompatibilities, we're even quicker to think in terms of 'limitations'. All of these can be present, and when they are, they can generate conflicts between people. What are we to do about them?

In the egocentric world, conflicts are read from only one perspective: mine. I have my reasons, my motives, and my wounds, and I interpret all problems or clashes with others from my own standpoint. I don't often stop to think that others also have their reasons, their motives and their wounds, and that very often, if I knew them, I'd get a bit more perspective when analysing situations.

It's very human for situations of friction and confrontation to arise between people. Circumstances and character all play a role in this from specific friction to vague likes and dislikes. We experience this in many areas. Perhaps the most complicated are the family and the workplace, though they're not the only settings in which such conflicts occur.

There are some faulty ways of dealing with conflicts, which only succeed in postponing problems, meaning they will inevitably come back later.

One is denial. Some people spend their lives avoiding uncomfortable situations, avoiding friction, and agreeing with anyone in front of them, even if this means agreeing with different people who hold incompatible views.

Denial may be comfortable, but it means not facing problematic situations, and sometimes it means adding more water to a reservoir so that when the dam finally bursts, it causes much more damage.

Another faulty way of avoiding conflicts is going at them indirectly. I have a conflict with you, and I talk about it to everyone except you. I don't talk to you, but I talk about you to whoever wants to listen to me. Normally, this type of discourse is full of complaints, gossip, bitter criticism and probably generalisations, which, if I chose to speak to you directly, I would have to express very differently.

So the challenge is to learn how to manage conflict. An in-depth discussion of methods of conflict management would be enough to fill entire books, but we need to focus on at least the following three points.

First, we have to be able to learn to live with friction, to have different points of view or even to discuss specific aspects of life without turning these differences into personal confrontation. Or, put another way, we have to be able to accept a flat contradiction without taking it as an insult or seeing it as a sign of a problem or personal animosity. Many conflicts arise unnecessarily from an incorrect reading of another person's words.

Second, we have to learn to read conflicts. This has to do with what was pointed out previously about discovering that the other is someone else and has his or her own story. There are so many elements at play in cases of friction between people that simply jumping to conclusions without knowing the data, without trying to unravel the reasons or without listening to other readings of the same reality, easily leads us to act out of prejudice (in the purest sense of pre-judgment).

A quarrel often masks a cry for help. An angry reprimand can be the result of the person being hurt by someone they love. Apparent antipathy is often a barrier to hide a person's insecurity.

Thirdly, when we have to face or try to deal with conflicts, the best way in most cases is to go directly to the person or people concerned. This does not guarantee solutions. Sometimes the conditions simply aren't right for us to be able to dialogue peacefully or find a solution to complex situations. But such an attempt certainly has more chances of success than gossip, distant contempt or violently upping the ante.

Learning to see the other in his or her need

Everything in our consumer society is geared towards increasing our desires. We have let ourselves get caught up in a cycle that only works if people are constantly dissatisfied with what they have. When we manage to reach a goal, fulfil an objective, get something we've been wanting for a long time, we spend a shorter and shorter period enjoying them before asking, 'What next?' And I'm not even talking here about planned obsolescence, about the products we use that become outdated before we've been able to enjoy them. I'm talking about fashions, which change so rapidly that we're constantly being bombarded with new offers. I'm talking about the endless series of new experiences, about an entertainment culture that replaces quality with quantity. A good example is what is happening with streaming, the increasing number of audiovisual productions, series, films, documentaries to be consumed and forgotten more and more quickly. I am also talking about the lack of time we spend on evaluating, valuing and enjoying what we've experienced, and about how even in personal relationships, this same culture of using and changing is spreading. All this means that, if we're not careful, we're constantly focusing on our own needs, because we are always longing for something we don't have. There's always something else, something that becomes an object of desire.

One simple question can help us change our perspective and get outside of our own appetites. A question addressed to others, not ourselves: 'What do you need?' As simple as that. So real, and so deep. If we're incapable of thinking that there are needs beyond our own, our drift towards selfishness is unstoppable.

Let me give an example.

I've often walked sections of the Camino de Santiago, in northern Spain, on pilgrimage with groups of young people. It's a formative experience, an inner and outer journey, and is somewhat demanding. A few years ago, on one of these pilgrimages, the following incident took place. I was with a large group, almost twenty young people of university age – between eighteen and twenty-five. It was the second-to-last day. It was very hot, and we'd walked almost thirty kilometres on a gruelling trek. We'd stopped for a snack and were lying down, dozing, having a bit of a rest before getting back on the road. There were still about five kilometres of a long climb to reach the hostel where we would sleep that night. In the hostels along the way the beds fill up as the pilgrims arrive. I'd already told them that the hostel we were making for didn't have that many beds, and some of us would possibly have to sleep on the floor that night.

While we were resting there, three pilgrims passed us, two women and a man. They were much older than our group. They looked tired. One of the women was also walking quite slowly; everything in her movements indicated that she had a sore point or blister that was making it difficult. These things are to be expected on the road, and you have to accept them and deal with them. The three of them greeted us cheerfully, and the young people responded encouragingly, 'Courage!' 'Have a good walk!' 'See you at the hostel!' The three pilgrims continued on their way.

About five minutes later, two more pilgrims passed by and, almost immediately, another one.

At that point, one of the young men in our group exclaimed, sounding alarmed, 'What if all the beds get taken before we get there?' It was as if he had given a signal, had put into words what many were thinking. Instantly everyone sprang to their feet and began putting on their backpacks, talking about how they were going to quicken their pace to get to the hostel first, overtaking the people who had passed us on the way. To be honest, I couldn't believe what I was hearing. Thank goodness we were a Christian group and that every day at Mass we talked about our neighbours and so on. However, at that moment of decision, there was neither neighbour nor priorities for them. There was only a huge ego that shouted, 'I'm exhausted, and I want to sleep on a bed tonight.'

Only when we were about to start walking did I explode, with some vehemence, 'Are you seriously going to rush to overtake those people and corner the beds for yourselves? Haven't you learned anything?' The more I talked, the more indignant I became. The surprise with which they received my outburst gave way to timid attempts at explanation and finally to a somewhat guilty silence. They weren't bad people at all. Just a group of young men and women who, in a moment of stress, thought only about their own needs. Perfectly understandable. But that's exactly where we must be on our guard, because that's the trap of the egocentric viewpoint. It turns us in on ourselves and prevents us from perceiving the more complex reality and of thinking of others when we act.

People just need to be encouraged to look outside themselves, to find another perspective. Of course, when we caught up with those three pilgrims, all of my group were quick to offer help, to encourage them on the climb, to accompany them on the last stretch, to carry their backpacks and, once we reached the hostel, to make sure that the older people were well settled before even thinking about where they were going to sleep themselves.

All it took was to remind them that in our shared life, in addition to being aware of what we need, it's essential for us to look around and ask ourselves what other people might be needing.

Learning to take action to help others

The above example leads to a further lesson. It isn't enough to see. It isn't enough to realise. It isn't enough to interpret situations correctly. We need to do all of that, but it still isn't enough. There is one more step that must be taken on the path to mature relationships: once we have seen the need, to be able to take action.

Here we enter into tricky territory. I can't go through life as a saviour of the world. There are so many people, so many stories, that I'd be overwhelmed: they're too much for me. If I try and respond to every wound, every lack, every problem, I'll end up exhausted, and I won't get very far. The world is full of people who badly need help, time, company, money, attention – and so many other things. And the fact is that one person can't do everything.

Even if there is a certain impulse to help in certain circumstances, it will always fall short of reality. Think of the outbursts of solidarity in the face of a humanitarian disaster. There's a major earthquake, a war breaks out, a tsunami devastates some area of the world, and solidarity campaigns are immediately launched. Everyone wants to help. And in fact, we don't need to wait for events like those to hit the headlines. Today, as you read this, there are countless drastic situations that need all the support possible.

Compassion, the awareness that there are many people in need of a helping hand at any given moment, begins much closer to home. People are in need not far from our home, in our street, in our town or city. There, all around us, is where we can begin to hone our sensitivity.

When we perceive the pain, the longings and the urgent need of some-one nearby is when we find ourselves faced with the choice of taking action or passing by on the other side.

Years ago, back in 2008, two events occurred simultaneously in Spain that hit the headlines. First, a security camera at the entrance of a hotel in Majadahonda recorded how a young man appeared to be mistreating his partner. Then another man intervened, trying to defend the woman. The aggressor reacted by hitting the would-be defender violently, and he was left in a coma.

Around the same time, a scene captured by the security camera of a metro in Barcelona came to light. There were three people in a metro carriage. A girl was being harassed by a young man, who was insulting her and visibly provoking her; it was later discovered that he was mak-ing xenophobic remarks. Although the situation was becoming more and more violent, another young man sitting at a distance refrained from intervening. He looked uncomfortable, gazed at the ground, and as soon as he had the chance he left the carriage.

Immediately public opinion passed sentence. The man in the first case was a hero. The man in the second case was a coward. It would certainly be useful to know more of the context, to see different possible inter-pretations and to know if everything really was as shown by the images. But let's assume that yes, we are basically seeing two similar situations and different reactions to them.

The convergence of both stories made me think a lot, because it seemed to me to be a very graphic image of the difference between act-ing and not acting.

From the comfort of our home, from an armchair watching the news – as in 2008 – or today from the screen of a mobile phone and through social networks, it's easy to interpret, judge, and criticise or praise other people's actions, or to boast about how we would inter-vene without hesitation. We are spectators acting as judges, but the question that haunted me when I saw those scenes was, 'What would I have done?' I know what I would want to be able to do, if I ever found myself in a situation like that. I would want to be able to intervene, to take risks, to stand up. I would want to be brave and not cowardly.

However, isn't this what actually happens so often and in so many similar situations? How often is omission the comfortable or prudent response to cases in which we could actually intervene? How often do we look down so as not to see, cross the street so as not to find ourselves face to face with someone else's need, or tell ourselves that it's impossible to help, instead of asking ourselves if it really is impossible, or if it's simply that we have other priorities.

We can't fight for all causes. We can't defend all trenches. We can't respond to all needs. But I think that maturing implies accepting that the world cannot be just a personal refuge, that relationships cannot be built on indifference, and that, although we can't respond to all of other people's needs, we'll have to find our own personal, unique way of complicating our lives with someone and for someone.

Learning to look deeply

Basically, joining up all the lessons sketched above requires the ability to look deeply into the reality of things and people. For me, Etty Hillesum provides an example of just that ability. She was a Dutch Jew who kept a diary during the Second World War and the Nazi occupation of Holland. She was imprisoned in Westerbork and then sent to Auschwitz, where she was killed. Her diary shows enormous perspicacity and sensitivity in grasping different situations and always trying to understand people. On 25 February 1942 she was summoned to the Gestapo headquarters in Amsterdam and described the scene as follows.

> Very early on Wednesday morning a large group of us were crowded into the Gestapo hall, and at that moment the circumstances of all our lives were the same. All of us occupied the same space, the men behind the desk no less than those about to be questioned. What distinguished each one of us was only our inner attitudes. I noticed a young man with a sullen expression, who paced up and down looking driven and harassed and making no attempt to hide his irritation. He kept looking for pretexts to shout at the helpless

Jews: 'Take your hands out of your pockets ...' and so on. I thought him more pitiable than those he shouted at, and those he shouted at I thought pitiable for being afraid of him. When it was my turn to stand in front of his desk, he bawled at me, 'What the hell's so funny?' I wanted to say, 'Nothing's funny here except you', but refrained. 'You're still smirking', he bawled again. And I, in all innocence, 'I didn't mean to, it's my usual expression.' And he, 'Don't give me that, get the hell out of here', his face saying, 'I'll deal with you later.' And that was presumably meant to scare me to death, but the device was too transparent.

I am not easily frightened. Not because I am brave, but because I know that I am dealing with human beings and that I must try as hard as I can to understand everything that anyone ever does. And that was the real import of this morning: not that a disgruntled young Gestapo officer yelled at me, but that I felt no indignation, rather a real compassion, and would have liked to ask, 'Did you have a very unhappy childhood, has your girlfriend let you down?' Yes, he looked harassed and driven, sullen and weak. I should have liked to start treating him there and then, for I know that pitiful young men like that are dangerous as soon as they are let loose on mankind. But all the blame must be put on the system that uses such people.[16]

I find this example fascinating: this was someone who was capable of going deeper than surface impressions. She did not stop at appearances, even when they were threatening ones. She possessed an unusual degree of empathy, even for a person who was being aggressive towards her at that very moment.

The question here is whether or not we will acquire the same gaze as Etty's in time. Whether the capacity to be open to the other will come

16. Etty Hillesum, *An Interrupted Life: the Diaries and Letters of Etty Hillesum 1941–43* (Bath: Persephone Books, 1999), pp. 104–105.

as we get older, or whether we may spend our whole lives looking at people and things through filters without ever escaping from the bubble or prison of mirrors.

Further questions present themselves: is it worth trying to acquire that depth of gaze, or not? What will we gain by it? What will it bring us? Won't it make life more complicated?

I think the honest answer to the first question, of whether such a penetrating view comes as we get older, is no: the mere passage of time doesn't guarantee a capacity to open up to the other. Life is a school, but we have to pay attention to be able to learn anything. It doesn't just depend on our sensitivity, ability or character. It's also a matter of interest and will. Even the most adult of adults can get trapped inside a bubble or spend their whole life seeking to see their own reflection in other people without ever being able to open themselves to the other and his or her situation.

Regarding the second question, whether this depth of gaze will bring us any advantage, or whether it will just lead to more problems, the answer is that it brings the capacity for a real encounter with the other, just as he or she is. And that makes interpersonal ties much deeper and at the same time much freer. It also brings clarity, knowledge, the sort of wisdom that acts as an antidote to stupidity. All too often, people spend their lives fighting against imaginary enemies, analysing others by attaching miserably inadequate labels to them or loving or hating externals without even thinking of getting inside the complexity of the life behind the façade. How pitiful to spend life in that state of blindness, when we could learn to look into people's depths!

Finally, the ability to look deeply at the other is a remedy for loneliness. Among other reasons, because it awakens genuine interest in life, in human beings, beyond ourselves. We learn to understand and appreciate other stories, and we discover similarities and motivations that otherwise we'd know nothing about.

In the centre of your life there is not a solitary dancer on a bare stage. What you need to be is a person who is learning to interact, to relate to others, to care for and give yourself to the other, but also to let yourself be cared for and to receive love from the other. And your dance should be a story not just a single moment frozen in time: a story of battling, surpassing, effort, emotions and lessons learned.

Even when you dance alone – and you sometimes will – there are other people around you. Their stories are interconnected with yours. And you know that they were there in your past, and are there in the present, however far off they seem; and in the future, as soon as a bend in the road brings a change of scene, they'll still be there.

9

Great Desires Don't Die Away

When the Chilean Jesuit Cristobal Fones looked back at his younger self, he told him, 'Great desires don't die away.' The first time I read that, it really made me think. What did he mean by 'great desires'?

Great desires

One of the most worthwhile experiences that life has to offer is that of finding our own place in the world. We get to a point where we feel we've completed one stretch of the journey, and we can say, 'Now I know where I want to be', even though we haven't got there yet; and we have the sensation that that desire is there to stay.

This happens from infancy onwards. Our great desires begin to take shape when we're still quite small. Our imagination begins to take flight, and we form longings and ambitions. And we also begin dreaming about the future.

It's true that different generations have different ambitions. When I was a child, nobody wanted to become an influencer, because they didn't even exist (or at least not as we have them now). Now, however, many kids imagine themselves being hugely popular with thousands or millions of followers on virtual platforms, creating trends while playing or commenting on the latest digital news. Many teenagers take all kinds of photos, acting as catwalk models in their living room or anywhere else that comes to mind, thinking about becoming the idols of the masses. And some even achieve it. In my time, the desires were different, although just as fanciful: we aimed to be Olympic athletes, soldiers, Hollywood actors accepting an Oscar or Top Gun pilots.

Some of these stereotypes are part of life for several generations, and others go out of fashion with cultural changes. Then you leave childhood behind, and ideas and horizons diversify. Someone asks, 'What do you want to be when you grow up?', and the answers start to vary and include the most personal ambitions, professional ones, existential ones ... There are teenagers who already know they want to be doctors, or who see themselves as barristers in court, or who tell you what country they want to live in because they've been captivated by this or that series. Some dream of having a family or leaving a mark in a way they already see as possible. As you enter into young adulthood, the life you would like to have begins to take shape.

The fact is that behind these images are the great desires that gave rise to them: to succeed, to be popular, to be loved, to be happy, to be rich, to do what you like, to be comfortable with yourself, to find love. These and other intentions are easily recognisable and shared by many people, although hopefully they're not the only ones.

If your upbringing and education included religious formation, personal sensitivity or an ethical purpose, then among the great desires you foster there will probably be some more, such as doing good, being a good person, leaving a mark on life, living in a meaningful way and even greater ambitions such as changing the world for the better.

I firmly believe that youth is the time when good desires have to be well formulated. It's the time when daydreams give way to resolutions, and it's very important for them to be appropriately designed, because they are what will take you forward.

I recognise that young people today find themselves in a very difficult world, and we older people do not fully comprehend this. We judge them from an unfair standpoint, comparing them with 'when we were young'. But things are not the same. Today's young people are not as lacking in idealism as we think, nor were we as idealistic as we may fondly imagine.

The world is in the midst of a revolution. In recent decades society has changed at a previously unimaginable speed and in unheard-of ways. Its dynamics force many young people into an unwanted situation of precariousness and prolonged adolescence, not by choice, but because it's

very difficult to become independent in today's economy and employ-
ment conditions. How can you become an adult, when you can't afford
to move out of your parents' house even if you're earning a salary? How
are you going to risk having a child if you can't get a permanent job?
How can you feel like an adult in a world where you're still treated like
a teenager?

Great desires involve the long term. They aren't instant goals or resolutions for one afternoon. They take time, sometimes a lifetime. They're
shaped throughout your personal story: a story of projects, struggles,
intuitions that you then make specific and practical.

When great desires almost hurt, because you see how impossible it
is for them to materialise, then it's understandable if you're tempted to
keep the bird in hand and let the thousands of birds that you could have
in your head or heart fly away. Or, to put it another way, it is understandable that some people choose to do without great desires and settle for
small, short-term goals. But reducing your desires to a feeble pragma-
tism means accepting defeat.

You have to avoid the temptation to settle for small personal desires: I
want my drink, my game with friends, my boring weekend, my gym, my
sex with no love story behind it and no future, my favourite series,
my cat, my bit of volunteering to make me feel good about myself and
my little, private chapel. I want a nice summer holiday with plenty of
photos and parties and affordable trips to visit people. And with that,
I'm content ... Maybe those dreams are more easily attainable and offer
protection against disappointment, but they also make for a very flat,
dull existence.

I think we always need to fight for our great desires. Don't settle for
small dreams. Youth, as I said before, is the time to define great desires.
That is why when we're young we question ourselves about our place
in the world.

Our personal vocation is the way our great desires materialise. For
example, for Christians who practise their faith, even minimally, the
Gospel can become part of their great desires. The Gospel offers a wide
spectrum of ambitions and ideals. Doing good, practising mercy, being
happy (in the way the Beatitudes describe), loving our neighbour,

feeding the hungry, clothing the naked, relating to God, feeling loved, being able to make sense of whatever suffering may come our way … All these would be great desires. Now they must be made specific in some way in each individual's own path.

The same is true of other great desires, whether altruistic or not: finding love, doing good, defending the planet, fighting injustice, telling stories, changing society, channelling creativity. At some point, we all have to try to give a realistic answer to this question, 'So how will this ideal of yours actually materialise in your life?'

Defend your passion against the passage of time

There's something great about daring to dream big. It's the idea of desiring ambitiously and pushing your desires a bit further than the safe limits. Your ambition can take on a definite shape when you're still young. I don't think it's 'idealism' in the sense of unreality. I get a bit cross when people talk about young people being very idealistic. It seems to imply that they're deluded and that growing up means giving up on idealism and becoming pragmatic, sceptical or both.

Dreaming big means not being content with inadequate views. It means believing in your own possibilities and being convinced that everyone has talents far beyond what we often put into play.

The moment of formulating your own calling, of discovering the place where you want to be in the world, is probably the moment when you take a definitive step towards adult life. It's not that you grow older (that happens over years), but you grow on the inside.

Then the overarching narrative is filled out with specific details, step by step. Love becomes a reality, with names, connections and specific shared projects. If you dreamed of a type of activity where your life found meaning, it now materialises as a job, a profession or a mission. In other words, your personal vocation begins to become a commitment and takes root. Do your great desires fade away? They shouldn't. They come down to earth, land on firm ground, which is different.

I like the image of fire and embers. When you want to barbecue meat, you don't put it over the flames. You have to wait, though the fire is necessary. In fact, the initial fire is showy; its flames dance and catch the eye. However, the wood or charcoal has to burn for a little, and when it has become glowing embers, that's the time to put the meat on.

I think that this idea of great desires is similar. It is a more definite shape. It's a humbler option, and it comes when the first flames have died out. And it's also the time of a different fruitfulness.

If someone tells you that great desires fade away, and that over the years you will wake up, or worse, become disillusioned – don't believe them. Perhaps there are people who have that experience and who end up viewing the world, and their own lives, sceptically, but your great desires can equally become a motivating force that draws you on. Your desires are still there but understood in a different way. They continue to encourage, inspire and stimulate you. They continue to define you a little.

To use the image of music, it's as if you've found the score, and now you have the chance to play it, bring it to life. You choose which instruments you're going to play it on, and perhaps it changes, grows, goes through quiet passages and fortissimo ones. But it's there like the soundtrack of your life.

I would put it like this: 'Defend your passion against the passage of time.' If someone tells you that you can do everything, try out everything and experience everything, don't believe that either. Life goes by too quickly. We shouldn't stress or agonise over it, but it goes by quickly, because we only have one.

Once again, cinema helps unpack certain ideas. *Facing Windows*, directed by Ferzan Özpetek, is my favourite film. It has so many different angles and skilfully evokes love, life and the passage of time. I've often quoted its thesis that all lives seem better if viewed from the window opposite. In this case, it's a different idea that grabs me. I'm fascinated by the friendship between Giovanna and Davide. Giovanna is a woman who is entering her forties and feels dissatisfied with her life. She always wanted to be a pastry chef, but has given up on her dreams and contented herself with working as an accountant on a chicken farm.

One day, Giovanna and her husband, Filippo, find Davide, an elderly man, disoriented and confused, on the street. They can't figure out where to take him and end up looking after him for a few days in their apartment. A delicate friendship begins between Giovanna and Davide. When he finally regains his memory, it turns out that he's a well-known pastry chef, and he goes back home. One day Giovanna goes to visit him. And while the two of them are cooking, she expresses her regret for her abandoned dream. It is then that Davide talks to her about the importance of taking care of what one is passionate about in life and not letting it fade away. He says forcefully, 'You've let your passion become a hobby.' That's the key. There are aspects of life that we cannot and should not reduce to mere hobbies or daydreams, because they are in reality what takes us forward, what helps us define who we are. These are the great passions that we must defend against the passing of time.

Today, advertising tries to tell us that we can try out every kind of life there is, and that since life is so very short we shouldn't waste time by tying ourselves down to any one thing; instead it's better to skip from emotion to emotion, from experience to experience, without stress or sadness. But that's not real.

We each live only one life. We have to make decisions, choose paths and stake our bets, and there will also necessarily be times of struggle and things we have to renounce ... but all of that is worth it when we know why we are doing what we do.

That's what's called meaning. The meaning of your life is its direction, its scope and its desire. That meaning enables you to move forward on sunny days but also on stormy ones. That meaning is the answer to the question, 'What about you, what do you live for? What do you want? What are you looking for?' This meaning is what enables you to say, one day, 'I finally know who I am.'

Even more than meaning, though, I like to talk about passion. It is that which gives you a goal to make for. It motivates you, excites you, moves you to make your decisions. Your passion will sometimes be projects, people, knowledge or a mixture of everything. I hope that in life we can each find a ruling passion that drives us. What's more, I hope it's a passion shared with others, people with whom we can forge deep bonds, more necessary than ever in this world of fragile or merely virtual relationships.

Even having that passion, there will be times when you think about the many paths you didn't choose. You mustn't fool yourself. You can't live every life, experience or try out everything, and you don't need to. It's worth thinking carefully about what you choose and looking for people to share the path with, and then bet on it and them, and calmly fight for it with conviction, unafraid of the storms. That is defending passion from the passage of time and turning your passion into a life story.

10

Faith Matures too

To believe or not to believe, that is the question

'When I was a child, I spoke like a child, I thought like a child, I reasoned like a child; when I became a man, I gave up childish ways' (1 Cor 13:11).

After writing his famous hymn to love in his first letter to the Christians in the Greek city of Corinth, the apostle St Paul goes on to talk about the passage of time and how people change with the years. He may still be referring to love, which also has to learn to grow up. But perhaps we can think how something similar is true of faith. There is adult faith, just as there is adult atheism. And in the same way, there's childish faith and childish atheism.

Did you pray when you were little? It probably depends on how you were brought up and which school you went to. But if you did, you probably remember how different your prayer was then from the way it is now. Maybe it held a lot of ingenuousness, though also a huge degree of trust. You may have been unshakably certain that if you were good, God would treat you well, and also a bit scared that if you misbehaved, God would punish you. And you didn't worry too much about whether there was actually anyone there listening to your prayers.

All the questions and uncertainties come later, if at all. They're the result of your personal history, gaining a broader view of the world, your intellectual development, the choices that life confronts you with and perhaps also disappointments. They're also the result of contact with reality, your need for more depth and meaning, and making sense of the complexity of life, perceiving aspects that perhaps when you were younger weren't so evident: injustice, pain, love, suffering, happiness and the many ways to achieve it, the passage of time and death.

It's normal to have the faith of a child when you're little, or if, as a child, you don't believe, it's more because of the example of your elders than because you've wrestled with the issues underlying religious questions.

What should change as you grow up is learning to have an adult faith – or disbelief – as time goes on. Or, to put it another way, just as we hope to live through whole love stories, and not just a collection of unconnected present moments, we also hope for our life of faith to be a personal story that develops and deepens over time.

Today the same polarisation occurs around faith as other areas of life. For or against. Believing, committed apologists or militant atheists. And between the two extremes, many people who somehow feel they've 'been through all that', but without actually having given the question of faith a chance. I've sometimes said that for me the biggest problem with faith or sociological atheism is that so many people feel they know all about it, without ever having gone into it at all. People who assume either that God exists or that he does not exist, but who have never taken the time to reflect on it. Some time ago I expressed it as follows.

> There are lots of young people who want nothing to do with religion. Today, at least in Spain, many people think that if you're a believer, and especially a practising one, you can't be normal. 'Do you still go to Mass? What a nutcase.' 'You belong to a group where they talk about the faith? That's serious, it must be a sect, you've been brainwashed.' 'You believe in God? How last-century!' (or 'How stupid!'). 'How can you belong to that Church?' (where 'that Church' is just an impoverished caricature that bears no relation to the complexity, richness and depth of the real Church and its members).
>
> It's funny, because in many matters there's a politically correct tolerance – and I will say frankly that it's good to

respect diversity of attitudes, orientations, sensitivities, opinions etc. – but then it seems equally correct to be tremen-
dously intolerant of personal beliefs. Sometimes I'm amazed
at how people insult others – friends, even close ones, as well
– because of their beliefs. It hurts me that more often than
not, they start from worn-out stereotypes that generally show
a lot of ignorance of what's really at stake when we talk about
faith. You often meet young people who seem prematurely
disillusioned by everything, sceptical for no reason, having
given up without a fight.

Sometimes this challenges me, other times it saddens
me, and other times it stirs me to action. It challenges me,
because we must recognise, with a bit of self-criticism, the
many errors that we've made – and still make – when passing
on our faith. It saddens me, because I realise that quite often
people who reject religion have a two-dimensional view of
it based on prejudices, facile simplifications and stereotypes,
rather than on questions, searches and serious thought. It
stirs me to action, because it is a call to help people open up.
How can we help people realise that religion really has to do
with the deepest, most authentic, most meaningful things
that come into play in our lives: love, joy, loneliness, our
place in the world, suffering, death, the encounter between
people, freedom, risk, time and God?

How can we help people to set out on the path of doubt,
search and faith, when often their attitude is that of someone who has 'been there, done that' without ever having
really gone?[17]

To believe or not to believe, that is the question. And it's not easy.
How does one arrive at faith or at disbelief? It's the result of many personal experiences: on the one hand, the upbringing and education one

17. J. M. Rodríguez Olaizola SJ, 'Being back without having gone', pastoralsj.org, https://pastoralsj.org
/creer/931-estar-de-vuelta-sinhaber-ido.

has received, and on the other, experiences that one has in life. And on top of that, one's ability to question oneself about the meaning of one's story.

There's no definitive solution to the dilemma of faith. If one person starts to justify why it's reasonable to believe in God, someone else will immediately appear from the other direction, explaining why the really reasonable thing is to disbelieve in the silent God believers talk about. If someone speaks of mystery, someone else will say that that's just a lazy explanation by people who don't have the courage to accept the ultimate meaninglessness of life. If someone says they believe, someone else will oppose them with the insufficient argument of 'I'm more into science', as if to say that believers are superstitious and primitive in their view of reality.

The fact is that you can believe childishly and you can also opt for an uncritical atheism that hasn't asked any questions, and, similarly, you can believe or not believe in an adult way.

What changes? Childhood faith (or childish atheism) is acquired in that first stage of very basic education. You learn it in the family, in your home setting. At first you don't question it. You inherit it in the same way as you inherit other family traits, customs, habits and ways of speaking. You are lucky enough, or unlucky enough (depending on how you look at it), to be born into a believing home that transmits their shared faith to you or a home where faith no longer plays any role, and where they transmit rejection or indifference. And there are degrees of both. You may be born into a believing and practising home or into one where faith is assumed but not practised, or into a home where God is simply absent from the worldview and the conversation, or into one where he is mentioned all the time, but only to question or deny his existence. You may even be born into a family where some believe and others don't, and the scepticism of the ones who don't is a challenge to the way the believers practise their faith. Everything is possible. Everything is legitimate. And everything happens.

Some people never get beyond that. They stay forever at the level of those first impressions, which are uncritically integrated into their worldview. If you are one of them, you'll continue praying all your life with a shallow, unquestioning faith, or else rejecting the idea of God with an equally shallow, uncritical atheism plus, sometimes, a sort of intellectual superiority complex.

Even if, as people frequently do nowadays, you make the move from the belief you got from your family background to religious indifference, it can be the result of unthinking inertia. You reach an age when you realise that for many people faith is not part of their life, when friends question you about why you go to Mass, or when, out of rebelliousness, you decide to take a stand against family traditions, but even then you haven't made the transition to a personal, adult attitude.

The big questions are the gateway to adult faith

The gateway to adult faith or atheism is questions about meaning and purpose: questions that we must necessarily ask ourselves when trying to work out the meaning and sense of our own lives and the world we live in. Where do we come from? How do we understand time? Did the universe have a beginning? Did time? And if so, what is its origin? Does God exist? Does he have a will? What role do we play? Is our hunger and thirst for transcendence simply fear of death, or is it a calling to greater things? What lies beyond the scope of science? Is it possible that there is a God who created us voluntarily? Even more, can he communicate with us? And would he want to? Is there life beyond death, or do we simply disappear? Do good and evil exist? If so, what are they based on? Who sets the limits of what is permissable? Are faith and science opposed to each other, or are they complementary ways of perceiving reality?[18]

Faith is often accused of being incompatible with science. That shows ignorance of the importance that faith has had in the questions raised by scientists throughout history. Religion is commonly accused of

18. For all those who believe that science and religion do not dialogue, I would like to recommend the collection '*Ciencia y Religión*' published by the Loyola Communication Group under the Sal Terrae label. It is a series of deep, solid examinations of the main questions involved in the dialogue between religion and science, https://gcloyola.com/982-fe-y-ciencia. (Tr.: Or, in English, the five books in the 'Questioning Faith' collection published by the Good Book Company and the various books by Brendan Sweetman.)

rigidity and superstition but that is to ignore the enormous flexibility of religious thought in dialogue with science.

In the introduction to his reflection on the dialogue between religion and science, Brendan Sweetman summarises the need for this dialogue.

> One of the reasons religion and science is such an important topic today is because both subjects make crucial contributions in so many areas of our lives. In addition, much recent work in various scientific disciplines has raised a variety of philosophical, religious and moral questions which science as a discipline is generally not equipped to deal with. Recent work in such areas as evolution, genetics, astronomy, astrophysics (the study of the physical composition of celestial bodies), stem cell research and neurology, much of it made possible by impressive technological advances, has brought to the forefront in a dramatic way what philosophers often call 'ultimate questions'. These are questions about the underlying nature of reality, the cause of the universe, the meaning of life and even about morality.[19]

To believe or not to believe isn't a question of utility. The starting point should not be, 'What does faith bring me?' or, 'Why do I need it?' If it were, freely deceiving yourself into belief, because it would leave you calm or give you a sense of security, would be as valid as choosing not to believe.

Fundamentally it is about curiosity, the desire to know, the will to understand the world in which we live and the lucid choice to look at the truth. It is not a question of whether believing in a non-existent God gives my security, or whether believing in an unprovable God gives me piece of mind; it's about seeking the truth.

Leaving childish faith behind

Even in a specific religion such as Christianity, and even more so Catholicism, there can be a childish Christianity and an adult Christianity.

19. Brendan Sweetman, *Religion and Science* (London: Continuum / Bloomsbury, 2010), p. 2.

People whose Christianity is still childish are content all their lives with the level of religious knowledge taught before their First Communion.

They are afraid of doubt, and they dogmatise everything, even what is not dogma. They build elaborate structures on over-literal interpretations. They reject all doubt, just in case. They are incapable of presenting an argument without turning it into violent conflict or heresy. They reduce theology to simple dualism, dividing reality absolutely into good and evil. They reduce the life of faith to fulfilling rules and morality to practising obligations.

Nowadays another form of religious childishness is spreading. It confuses the experience of faith with feelings and reduces religious experience to a vague emotionalism. Believing, in this case, means experiencing some feel-good moments of religious effervescence, and it's perfectly compatible with completely opposite views and approaches in other areas of life. That is a very delicate concept, compatibility. When everything is compatible, our lives lose all consistency. The only criterion that matters is my will: what I want, when I want, the way I want. Or, even more inconsistent, my appetite: what I feel like, when I feel like, and the way I feel like. This is a huge trap: we fragment the faith and reduce it to easily-managed compartments of our own lives, in such a way that it's perfectly compatible with other approaches and life goals that are very far from the Gospel.

Faith grows as the person grows. I don't mean it necessarily increases, so that the older you grow, the more faith you have. You can be a child with enormous faith. It isn't a question of quantity. But, even so, faith can grow up. That means it learns to deal with complexities, with unresolved questions, with uncertainty, with realising that not everything has to be interpreted literally. You learn to distinguish between what is transcendent in a religion and what is the product of culture, history and shared heritage, more attributable to tradition than to revelation. You have to go through the disillusionment of a disenchanted world, coming to understand that it is not a magical world inhabited by spirits like those esoteric-type stories in some films and television series that have become fashionable.

After the disenchantment comes a new look capable of reading reality from the standpoint of faith. You understand that there is a spirit that acts, but you strip it of paranormal expectations. You can dare to speak of God's will, but you don't turn God into the great puppeteer who moves us all at whim like pieces on a board.

A few months ago there was an episode much featured on the networks that shows why a child's view is insufficient. A father posted a video on social media in which his young daughter – who was maybe five or six years old – described with horror her first visit to a cathedral. The girl describes her experience in these terms: 'Scary. Seriously scary. Baby Jesus tied to a post. A virgin with a sword stuck in her. A dead boy all bloody. Virgins locked up in prisons. It looks more like a house of horrors than a place for weddings.' The video immediately went viral and detractors of Catholicism piled in enthusiastically, wanting to show the girl's horror as irrefutable proof of the gory tone of the Catholic religion.

In reality, a child doesn't have to understand much more. It is the responsibility of adults to be able to explain to children, in terms that they can understand, the elements shown in Christian iconography: dedication, love, suffering, passion ... all the aspects of life that are included in it.

If the dictatorship of political correctness entered the field of Christian iconography, then we would have to replace cathedrals with enclosures nicely decorated with cartoon-style characters. But all that belongs to a child's world, not an adult's.

In praise of doubt

Perhaps the most significant element of adult faith or disbelief is the ability to accept doubt. The believer must accept a certain degree of uncertainty. We must accept a clear awareness that much of what we attribute to God is our own projection and that, in any case, our language is figurative, incomplete and approximate when we speak about God.

Doubt is not the exclusive property of believers. Non-believers must also recognise that they haven't been able to prove that God doesn't exist, and that therefore there are gaps in their worldview. Some, of course, object that it hasn't been possible to prove that blue unicorns don't exist or, for that matter, fairies, mermaids or elves; yet it's perfectly certain that they don't. The difference is that nothing in the world leads us to consider that the possible existence of a unicorn or other mythical creature resolves any question on the origin, meaning or destiny of the universe or life. On the other hand, the idea of God fills gaps that no other type of discourse has so far filled, so it is, at least, a hypothesis to consider.

So can non-believers also accept doubt? Personally I think that's the most mature thing to do. The opposite would be another form of dogmatism.

What does doubt offer us? Reasons to continue searching. The ability to dialogue with those who hold other points of view or defend other worldviews. The intellectual humility of not claiming to possess the whole truth, and consequently, of accepting the need for change. The possibility of taking risks, without demanding a degree of certainty that cannot be achieved.

Conclusion: Dancing with Time

After this long journey we've been taking through different aspects of life, to which the passage of time can bring maturity, depth and solidity, these final considerations aim to be a description of this dance that is life itself.

It's a privilege to know we're alive and also to know that time is one of the coordinates of our life and actions, that our different ages are part of the same story and to learn to value what each of them holds.

In this time when youth is idolised, and when it's so scary to step into adult life, I wanted to write a book for both young people and adults.

I would like to tell you young people to enjoy youth a lot. Enjoy it, which doesn't mean reducing it to having fun, although you can always be grateful for opportunities to have a good time. Enjoying means making the most of life's different aspects, deeply, passionately and meaningfully. When you have something to celebrate, celebrate. Set about forging strong bonds with the people who become important in your life. There are many fleeting experiences that you can take lightly, but be sure to experience intensely the ones that will leave a mark. And learn to distinguish one from the other. Learn. Open yourself to knowing the world, people, society. You won't be able to know everything, but don't be satisfied with superficiality or ignorance. Take risks while you search. Risk is part of life. Don't aim to try out everything, because it's impossible. But don't aim to always stay on the safe side either. Failure and success will be dance partners throughout your whole life story. It doesn't matter if they're there right now. It's better that way, because life is a school. Take care of yourself on the outside and inside but especially on the inside. And although you happen to live in a time when image is very important, laugh at it a little. Perfection isn't permanent, nor is imperfection a tragedy.

Trust me on this above all: time goes by very quickly. And we only have one life, even though some gurus of new technologies, humanisms and post-humanisms keep claiming to find a recipe for eternal life. So don't leave becoming an adult until too late. I know that to a large extent it's not your fault if you don't achieve adulthood sooner, nor is it because you don't want to. Society itself is making it increasingly difficult to achieve autonomy, independence and the responsibility that comes when you finally settle on a definite life project. But don't resign yourself. Don't let them tell you that you're still an adolescent, when you're not. Don't just let the years go by for the sake of convenience. Because a time may come when you discover, with regret, that it's got late without your realising it.

For those of us who can no longer call ourselves young, I would also like to share some thoughts: on maturity, on becoming adults, on settling into life. Don't be afraid to say, 'I'm old!' Instead laugh at this strange obsession with staying eternally young. What for? Regret for paths not chosen? Don't get caught up in that. A longing for experiences from a bygone era? The challenge is to learn to live through the things you meet when you are building your life, when you are bringing your desires into harbour, when you are putting down roots in some specific land (places, names, projects ...). Adult life is a stage of more nuances. And you carry much more baggage than you imagine. Not only, or mainly, a heavy load, although there may be some of those. It is above all a load of experiences, learning, names, words of love, desires, knowledge ... Appreciate them and keep them. They are a treasure.

I've spoken throughout this book of the many battles that occur in life. Being an adult doesn't mean you've won all of them. It means you've dared to fight them, knowing that you're moving forward, bruised but confident. That defeats and victories have become a school, and you have learned something from both. If I tell young people to laugh at their 'image', I tell you to laugh even more. Perhaps because you already know that summer is followed by autumn, and that your body will ask you for a break and remind you that you are finite and that you will have more than one scar – on the outside and on the inside – that tells your story. Don't lose your curiosity and thirst for knowledge. Don't turn routine into conformity. Let the awareness that time is finite make you equally grateful and free. Don't waste too much time on boredom. Be critical but not doom-mongering. Remember the reasons that motivated you to take certain steps one day.

This last part goes for everyone, young and old, those who have already lived a lot and those who are still starting. Dance with time! Imagine a large dance hall. I don't know why, but I always think of the enormous hall of a large train station. Imagine that when you came in at one end, everyone was already dancing. The music is a combination of noise, conversations, laughter, tears, beliefs, imagination, beauty … All converging in a strange composition that each person hears with different nuances.

You come in, and at first you hardly know how to move, but the music – which is life, science, faith, joy, love – envelops you, and you can't help but start dancing. At first you imitate the way others move. Then you let go and start improvising and create your own steps. You move through that huge hall. You change. You grow. Sometimes you join a circle that's cheering on an exceptional dancer. Maybe the exceptional dancer, for a while, is you. But you don't stay there for long either.

You dance alone or with others. Some dance partners stay behind. Others keep by you. The rhythm also varies. There are moments of thunder and others when you have to strain to catch a faint melody. But you keep moving forward.

Until one day you reach the platform and board the train that will take you to an unknown destination. You will depart, but the dance will continue behind you, because at the already distant end of the hall people will continue to arrive, claiming their time and their place.

Dancing with time means accepting that it's fleeting and understanding that we're part of a stream of names that didn't begin with us and won't end with us. We join a dance that is in progress, and we incorporate our own steps, sensitivity and energy.

Don't stop dancing: with others, with yourself, with the world and with God.

One day you will dance with time.

You'll turn yesterday into a school.
Your luggage
carries beloved names,
victories, defeats,
wounds and scars,
familiar smells,
places to travel through
from memory to memory.
The music of the past is memory.

You'll dance with the present,
agendas, hurry, obligations, noise …
sometimes peacefully and other times restlessly,
some days your calm smile
will infect whoever sees you.
On others, your worry will become
a hesitant step.
But dance,
don't give up trying.
Now is the time
to take life seriously.

The future also awaits you,
full of possibilities
and paths to follow.
There, faces are waiting
that you can't yet see,
new crossroads,
looming battles,
and reasons for joy.
Hope, that is its music.

And God?
God is the lord of time.
Companion in your story.
Partner in the dance.
Creator of the music within.

It's time.
Let the dance begin.

Foreword by Brian Grogan SJ

Dancing with Loneliness

José María R. Olaizola SJ

Messenger MJP Publications

www.messenger.ie

About the Translator

Helena Scott holds an M.A. in Classics and a Diploma in Translation. She has translated a number of books and many academic articles, and continues to work in the fields of translating, proof-reading and teaching.